BRITISH DREADNOUGHT
VS
GERMAN DREADNOUGHT

JUTLAND 1916

MARK STILLE

First published in Great Britain in 2010 by Osprey Publishing,
Midland House, West Way, Botley, Oxford, OX2 0PH, UK
44–02 23rd St, Suite 219, Long Island City, NY 11101, USA
E-mail: info@ospreypublishing.com

A CIP catalogue record for this book is available from the British Library.

Print ISBN: 978 1 84908 167 2
PDF e-book ISBN: 978 1 84908 168 9

Page layout by: Ken Vail Graphic Design, Cambridge, UK
Index by Sandra Shotter
Typeset in ITC Conduit and Adobe Garamond
Maps by Bounford.com
Originated by PDQ Digital Media Solutions
Printed in China through Bookbuilders

10 11 12 13 14   10 9 8 7 6 5 4 3 2 1

Osprey Publishing is supporting the Woodland Trust, the UK's leading woodland
conservation charity, by funding the dedication of trees.

Acknowledgements
The author would like to thank the staff of the Naval History and Heritage
Command Photographic Section (formerly the US Naval Historical Center) for
their assistance in procuring the photographs used in this book. Special thanks go
to Keith Allen and friends who graciously reviewed the text and clarified many
technical points for the author.

Dedication
The book is dedicated to Bill Karwacki

CONTENTS

INTRODUCTION

Since 1805, the Royal Navy had reigned supreme on the world's oceans. Though this supremacy was challenged at times, by the turn of the 20th century the Royal Navy was facing its most serious challenge in some 100 years. This challenge came in the form of a united Germany and its growing industrial strength. As the two most powerful industrial powers in Europe, Germany and Britain were engaged in trade competition; by the turn of the century this competition was beginning to take a more alarming turn in the form of a naval rivalry.

With its global empire and worldwide trading interests, Britain needed a large navy to maintain its position and power. What concerned the British was the development of a sizeable navy by a continental power with no naval tradition and, seemingly, no need for such a force. The reasons why Germany became a maritime power remain controversial even today. Many in Germany felt that a great power, as Germany was becoming, had to possess a strong navy to bolster its status and to support and defend its trading interests. There is also evidence that the drive for a powerful navy had its roots in German internal politics. When the State Secretary of the Imperial Naval Office, Admiral Alfred von Tirpitz, began to agitate for a large navy he found fertile ground and a large degree of support.

In 1897, Tirpitz outlined a plan to increase the size of the German Navy to provide political and military leverage against Germany's most dangerous enemy, Britain. The goal for 1905 was to possess a fleet of 19 battleships. This force was the so-called 'risk fleet' – a fleet powerful enough to act as a deterrent against a British attack, by threatening the Royal Navy with such severe losses that it would lose its maritime supremacy. If the British were allayed by German promises that this fleet was purely defensive, there was no doubt about the purpose of the Second German Naval Law of June 1900. The law provided for a fleet of 38 battleships, organized into four

squadrons of eight ships each along with two fleet flagships and four reserve battleships. This dramatic German decision to challenge Britain's naval supremacy not only put the Royal Navy on notice, but changed the direction of British foreign policy. In order to maintain its commanding naval position and contain Germany, the British abandoned their policy of isolation. From 1902 to 1907, agreements were reached with Japan, France and Russia. Thus, when an event in Europe set off the powder keg between the two opposing power blocks, the British were virtually ensured of being dragged in against Germany. This consequence was the true legacy of Tirpitz's desire to build a large fleet. As Tirpitz's dream of a large German Navy was gaining favour in his homeland, the Royal Navy was undergoing a transformation, led by the controversial First Sea Lord, Admiral of the Fleet Sir John Fisher. As the Royal Navy's leader from 1904 to 1910, Fisher oversaw its transformation from the complacency of the world's dominant peacetime navy, to a force ready to conduct modern war. He directed that large numbers of obsolete warships be scrapped and that the fleet be concentrated in home waters to oppose the growing German fleet. The most dramatic of Fisher's plans was the introduction of a new type of warship based on his concepts of an all-big-gun warship. This ship, named *Dreadnought*, was so revolutionary that

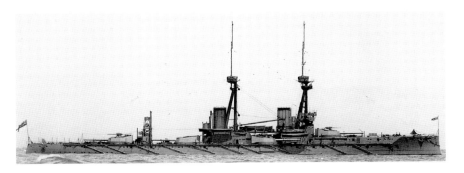

Bellerophon was a virtual repeat of *Dreadnought*. Armour was actually weaker, but one improvement was to move the foremast in front of the forward smokestack, reducing smoke interference in the gunnery control position. She served the entire war assigned to the Grand Fleet and was sold for scrap in 1922.

Naval balance, August 1914		
	Britain	Germany
Dreadnoughts		
In service:	22	15
Under construction:	13	5
Battlecruisers		
In service:	9	3
Under construction:	1	3
Pre-dreadnoughts	40	22

it made every other battleship obsolete. It was also a controversial move in Britain, as it wiped away the Royal Navy's existing advantage in battleships and levelled the playing field, thus providing the Germans with a chance to catch up. The advent of *Dreadnought* was followed by Fisher's pet project, the battlecruiser, which combined the hitting power of a battleship and the speed of a cruiser. The cost of this combination was a relative lack of armoured protection, which Fisher, incorrectly, believed could be compensated for with superior speed. The result of Fisher's revolution was that the strength of any navy was now measured in terms of the number of dreadnoughts it possessed. All battleships designed before *Dreadnought* were considered as 'pre-dreadnoughts' and were no longer fit for duties with the main battle fleet.

Fisher was willing to take the risk of radically changing the naval balance with the introduction of *Dreadnought* because he calculated that British shipyards could out-build any rival. Fisher was correct in this belief. By the start of the war in August 1914, the Royal Navy had established a firm superiority, as demonstrated by the table above.

NAVAL STRATEGY IN 1914

For both Britain and Germany, control of the North Sea was vital. After all the drama and expense of the great naval race between the two countries, the commanders of both navies expected a titanic naval clash shortly after war was declared. Yet the strategies on both sides ensured that such a clash between dreadnoughts would not occur for two years, and then by accident.

Traditionally, the Royal Navy preferred to institute a close blockade of its opponents to ensure that British shipping was undisturbed, and to maximize the

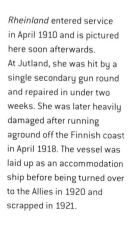

Rheinland entered service in April 1910 and is pictured here soon afterwards. At Jutland, she was hit by a single secondary gun round and repaired in under two weeks. She was later heavily damaged after running aground off the Finnish coast in April 1918. The vessel was laid up as an accommodation ship before being turned over to the Allies in 1920 and scrapped in 1921.

chances that an enemy would be brought to battle. By the 20th century, however, new naval technologies had made a close blockade too dangerous. The introduction of mines and torpedoes aboard submarines, torpedo boats and destroyers made it too dangerous to maintain large units close to enemy naval bases. Briefly, the Royal Navy considered the use of an 'observational blockade' centred on a point in the North Sea halfway between Germany and Britain, but even this was dismissed as impractical. When the British declared war on Germany in August 1914, they put in place a distant blockade with the aim of controlling the exits from the North Sea. The Grand Fleet was charged to conduct frequent sweeps into the North Sea to keep the German fleet in port and to assert control of the waters. The Channel Fleet, based around a number of pre-dreadnoughts, blocked the English Channel. Cruisers patrolled the area from the Shetlands to the Norwegian coast.

The Germans were counting on the British to try to impose a close blockade of the Heligoland Bight. The intention was that if the Royal Navy appeared close to German bases, U-boats, torpedo craft and extensive mine barrages would inflict losses on the numerically superior British until the German heavy units could engage the Grand Fleet at equal strength. Even if the Royal Navy did not attempt a close blockade, the Germans believed that the British would still commit light forces to watch the Heligoland Bight, and that the Royal Navy would be forced to support these forces. This situation would still offer the Germans ample opportunity to attrite the Grand Fleet until the odds had been evened. In the event that the battleships of the Grand Fleet remained near Scapa Flow (their main naval base) on distant blockade, the Germans felt they did not have sufficient strength to attack them at that location. This outcome is actually what happened when war began – the Grand Fleet went to its blockade station at Scapa Flow and no light units were committed to watch the German bases on the Heligoland Bight. The German naval staff had no plans to deal with this eventuality.

The commander of the Grand Fleet, Admiral Sir John Jellicoe, realized that he had a significant advantage in dreadnoughts over the Germans, but was worried about what he perceived as a critical German advantage in destroyers, as well as the mine and U-boat threat. These dangers reinforced his determination not to take the Grand Fleet too close to Germany's North Sea bases. The commander of the German High Seas Fleet was under orders from the Kaiser not to risk the fleet unless there was the likelihood of victory. Such an opportunity could only exist if the Grand Fleet had already suffered attrition or if the Germans found an opportunity to engage just a portion of the British warships. With both sides reluctant to commit their main fleets in anything but favourable circumstances, and both sides unlikely to believe that a given situation was favourable anyway, a major clash between fleets was going to be a matter of accident, not design.

CHRONOLOGY

1906
February   *Dreadnought* launched; all previous battleships now obsolete.

October   *Dreadnought* is completed, and begins sea trials.

1907
March   First German dreadnought, *Nassau*, launched. Three more units of this class follow.

July   British dreadnought *Bellerophon* launched, followed by two additional units of the same class.

1908
September   *St Vincent* launched; first ship in class of three.

1909
September   German dreadnought *Helgoland* launched; first ship in class of four.

September   *Neptune* launched; two near sisters launched following year.

1910
August   British 'super-dreadnought' *Orion* launched; all four ships in class carry new 13.5in gun.

1911
March   German dreadnought *Kaiser* launched; first of five in class.

October   *King George V* launched; first of four in class.

1912
October   *Iron Duke* launched; lead ship of four in class.

1913
March   Dreadnought *König* launched; lead ship of four.

October   Most powerful British dreadnought of World War I, *Queen Elizabeth*, launched; four more ships follow.

1914
August   Start of World War I.

Invincible was the first British battlecruiser completed in 1908. Built as dreadnought versions of the armoured cruiser, they relied on speed rather than armour. British admirals, however, found it too tempting not to put this large 12in-gun armed vessel in the battleline. The result at Jutland was the loss of three battlecruisers, including *Invincible*. In fairness, their loss was more attributable to the nature of British propellant powder than insufficient armour.

Westfalen leading a column of High Seas Fleet dreadnoughts before the war. She was the second German dreadnought to be commissioned. At Jutland, she was a member of I Battle Squadron, composed of Germany's oldest dreadnoughts.

November	*Royal Oak*, first ship in five dreadnoughts of the Royal Sovereign class, launched.

1915
February	*Bayern* launched, first German dreadnought with 15in guns, but she is not ready by the battle of Jutland.

1916
30 May	Battle of Jutland.
2230	Grand Fleet puts to sea.
31 May	
0100	German battlecruisers put to sea.
0200	German High Seas Fleet departs Wilhelmshaven.
1400	German and British ships investigate sighting of a Danish freighter.
1428	First shots of battle of Jutland between British and German light forces.
1548	German battlecruiser *Lutzow* opens fire; fire returned by British battlecruisers.
1603	British battlecruiser *Indefatigable* blows up. British dreadnoughts of 5th Battle Squadron open fire.
1626	Battlecruiser *Queen Mary* blows up. 'Run to the North' after British light cruisers spot High Seas Fleet.
1755	German light cruisers spot Grand Fleet.

1815	Grand Fleet begins to deploy into battle formation.
1825	Armoured cruiser *Defence* blows up.
1833	British battlecruiser *Invincible* blows up.
1833	Scheer orders first of three 'battle about-turns' to avoid growing fire of Grand Fleet.
1855	Second 'battle about-turn' puts High Seas Fleet into massed fire from British dreadnoughts.
1913	'Death ride' of the German battlecruisers assists escape of High Seas Fleet.
1916	Final 'battle about-turn' allows High Seas Fleet to break contact with Grand Fleet.
2110	Scheer orders High Seas Fleet to south-east to break through rear of Grand Fleet to return to base.
2230	High Seas Fleet encounters 4th Destroyer Flotilla; bitter close-range encounters ensue.
1 June	
0020	Armoured cruiser *Black Prince* engaged and sunk by German dreadnoughts.
0145	Germans encounter 12th Destroyer Flotilla.
0147	Battlecruiser *Lutzow* scuttled.
0202	Pre-dreadnought *Pommern* torpedoed and sunk with entire crew lost.
0520	Dreadnought *Ostfriesland* hits mine.
1500	High Seas Fleet returns to Wilhelmshaven.

DESIGN AND DEVELOPMENT

ADVENT OF THE *DREADNOUGHT*

On 2 October 1905, a revolutionary new warship was laid down in Portsmouth, England. The ship was launched in an incredible four months and was completed and ready to commence sea trials in an equally remarkable span of 365 days. The ship, named HMS *Dreadnought*, was so advanced that she immediately rendered every other existing battleship obsolete. What made this ship so remarkable? Most significant, *Dreadnought* was the first 'all-big-gun' ship. Previous battleships carried an array of weapons, usually a main battery of 12in guns supported by several other batteries of lesser size. Because actions were conducted at fairly short ranges, the smaller guns supporting the slow-firing main guns were perfectly adequate for penetrating the more lightly armoured areas of an enemy battleship. Yet as improved fire-control procedures pushed engagement ranges out farther, the effectiveness of the smaller guns began to diminish. Additionally, fire control was actually made more difficult by the impossibility of distinguishing the splashes of the 12in guns from any of the ship's other guns.

The merits of the all-big-gun ship were obvious not only to the British. The Italians and the Americans were also exploring this concept, and the US Navy had already designed and been authorized two all-big-gun battleships earlier in 1905. However, the Royal Navy under the energetic and far-sighted Fisher was the first to take action with the construction of *Dreadnought*. Fisher ordered that the new steam turbine powerplant, still not perfected, was also placed on *Dreadnought*, giving her a speed of 21 knots and making her the fastest battleship in the world at the time.

Accompanying the advent of the *Dreadnought* was the introduction of Fisher's pet project, the battleship-cruiser. These ships, eventually known as battlecruisers, also featured an all-big-gun armament and the new steam turbines. The principal difference between them and a dreadnought was the provision of a lighter scale of armour protection. This reduced weight burden, combined with the turbines, gave the new battlecruisers a several knot speed advantage over dreadnoughts and all armoured cruisers of the day. The extra speed, Fisher believed, would act as a measure of protection. The battlecruisers possessed the pace and armament to hunt down and destroy the most powerful armoured cruisers of the period, while their speed gave them the option of withdrawing from action against a dreadnought with superior armament. This premise, however, was forgotten by both sides during the war, when the battlecruiser was forced to engage ships equipped with heavy armament. Given the battlecruiser's inferior protection, the results were predictable.

The 13.5in guns aboard *Emperor of India*, shown here, were formidable weapons. At 20 degrees elevation, they could throw a 1,400lb shell a maximum of 23,800 yards. A well-trained gun crew could fire almost two rounds per minute.

GERMAN GUNS

The German propensity to employ smaller guns resulted in an 11in gun (top) being fitted to the first class of German dreadnoughts. This gun was a high-velocity 45cal weapon. Most German dreadnoughts were fitted with dual 12in gun turrets (bottom). The only real difference between the two turrets was the different gun, with the 12in gun being longer. All German dreadnought main battery turrets were provided with a rangefinder, which can be seen on the turret roof. Unlike on British large-calibre turrets, the viewing port for the crew was fitted on the turret front to avoid blast damage from a turret fired above it. These turrets were heavily armoured; the heaviest armour was placed on the turret face and was up to 12in thick on some ships. The sides of the turret received a similar level of protection, but the tops and rear were given much less armour. Note the dark turret tops with the white circle used as a recognition aid to German aircraft and airships.

BRITISH GUNS

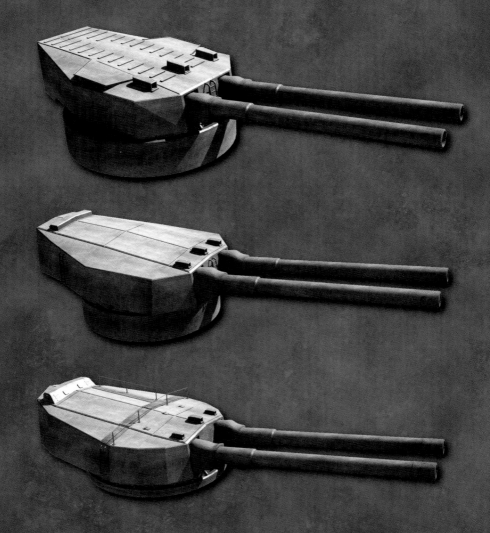

The 12in/45 gun turrets (top) aboard HMS *Dreadnought* and ships of the Bellerophon class were actually a carry-over from the last class of British pre-dreadnoughts. The turret was reliable in service and had a rate of fire of approximately two rounds per minute, per gun. It was heavily armoured with 11in of armour on the face and sides, 12in on the rear, but only 3in on the roof.

All three classes of 13.5in-gunned dreadnoughts, as well as two classes of battlecruiser, used the same 13.5in/45 dual turret (middle). The most successful British capital ship main armament was the 15in/42 gun turret (bottom) aboard ships of the Queen Elizabeth and Revenge classes,

as well as some late war battlecruisers. This gun was so reliable and accurate that it served through World War II. Armour on these dreadnought turrets was 13in on the face, 11in on the sides and rear, and 4–5in on the roof.

All British main battery turrets carried a rangefinder installed in the rear of the turret. Unlike on Germans ships, this rangefinder was used primarily as a back-up, since the ship usually controlled its main guns through a centralized control system. Note the provision of roof-top sighting hoods, which made the gun crew susceptible to blast damage if a superfiring turret fired over it.

DESIGN CONSIDERATIONS

Dreadnought designs are a fine balance between several competing factors. The foremost of these are firepower, protection and propulsion. Each factor carries with it weight and cost considerations. In general, British dreadnought designs tended to stress firepower. British battleships carried larger guns than their German counterparts, giving them greater firepower. Conversely, German battleship designers tended to emphasize protection at the expense of firepower. A major factor in the competing efforts to provide adequate protection was that after a certain point in the dreadnought race it was dictated to Royal Navy designers that an increase in beam was not possible due to the size of existing dry docks to accommodate the ships. The Germans had no such restrictions. Their battleships possessed a greater beam that in turn allowed for increased protective measures, which included greater subdivision and the inclusion of torpedo bulkheads.

FIREPOWER

The mainstay British naval weapon at the start of the dreadnought era was the 12in gun, dating back to 1893. In order to improve the muzzle velocity, range and penetration of this weapon, its barrel length had been expanded from 35 calibre to 50 calibre. At longer ranges, however, it was found that the latest versions had accuracy problems. The high muzzle velocity also had the effect of increasing wear and tear on the barrel, thus reducing gun life.

To solve this problem, the Royal Navy went to the 13.5in gun beginning with the Orion class of dreadnoughts. Most importantly, this gun provided for a much larger shell with improved penetration. The larger shell and increase in bore also permitted a lower muzzle velocity, which made for much greater accuracy and less barrel wear. The final development of Royal Navy pre-war dreadnought armament was the production of a 15in gun. Its combination of reliability and accuracy made it one of the best large guns ever developed by the Royal Navy. Because the muzzle velocity was comparatively low, the barrel life was also outstanding.

The German Navy's first dreadnoughts used an 11in gun that possessed a high muzzle velocity and thus outstanding range. It fired a relatively small shell, however, which limited its penetration. In their second class of dreadnoughts, the Germans introduced a slightly larger 12in gun. They clung to the 12in shell even as the British moved on to the 13.5in and finally a 15in shell, preferring the greater range and penetration against the higher barrel wear and reduced accuracy.

Although British dreadnoughts carried a larger main gun than their German opponents, this was not the case for the secondary armament. The Royal Navy used 4in guns from *Dreadnought* up through the King George V class. These were much criticized for being inadequate to deal with the growing size of torpedo boats and destroyers. The Royal Navy was unable to get a larger secondary armament due to the increased costs of mounting a 6in gun battery, and the views of Fisher who had

The mainstay German dreadnought weapon was the 12in gun mounted in double turrets, as seen here on *Kaiser* before the outbreak of war. The maximum elevation of the turret was 13.5 degrees, which gave a maximum range of 21,000 yards. After Dogger Bank, the Germans began a programme of increasing the elevation of their 12in turrets to 16 degrees, which translated to a maximum range of 22,300 yards. By Jutland, however, only *Prinzregent Luitpold* had been so modified. The hoists in German turrets were faster than those in British turrets, so the rate of fire for German turrets approached three rounds per minute.

advocated that capital ships should mount an all-big-gun armament. The Iron Duke class was the first to use a 6in gun secondary armament, and this weapon became standard on all subsequent designs. The German Navy adopted the 5.9in gun as their dreadnought secondary armament from the start.

Ostfriesland in 1920 under American control. This overhead shot presents a fine view of her main armament and part of her 5.9in casemate-mounted secondary armament. *Ostfriesland* was perhaps the most well-known German dreadnought because of the series of tests she endured in 1921. After being hit by 80 bombs of various sizes and 24 shells, she was finally sunk by Colonel Billy Mitchell on 21 July 1921 by six large bombs.

FIRE CONTROL

The true measure of a battleship's effectiveness is not the size and number of its guns, but its ability to hit its target. At short range, a shell follows a flat trajectory, which reduces the fire-control problem of compensating for the roll of the ship while pointing the gun at the target. As the range of guns continued to increase, the importance of effective fire control over greater distances was magnified. At longer ranges, the trajectory of the shell increases and a number of factors affect the accuracy of gunnery. By the outbreak of war, the Royal Navy had devised a very elaborate system of fire control. The basis for long-range fire was the use of a rangefinder to measure the distance from a gun to its target. The standard British battleship rangefinder was the 9ft-long coincidence rangefinder developed by Barr and Stroud. It was technically capable of providing ranges within 85 yards at 10,000 yards. As was later evidenced at Jutland, however, the accuracy of the rangefinder was much reduced in service due to light refraction and the heating of the rangefinder tube.

A rangefinder provided only the true range, however, not the gun range, which needed to include the distances of target movement and own ship's movement. Factoring in all these variables provided what is known as the range rate. To do this, the Royal Navy adopted an analogue computing device (known more commonly as the Dumaresq, after its inventor), which helped compute and check the range rate against other data. The range rate information was transmitted to guns electromechanically by means of a Vickers receiver-transmitter, which equipped all ships after *Dreadnought*. In 1912, the Admiralty adopted the Dreyer Table to provide a fairly comprehensive approach to fire control, allowing operators to visually compare ranges reported by rangefinders to a continuously evolving estimate of the range being sent to the guns. Unfortunately for the Royal Navy, the Dreyer Table was unable to contend with rapid changes of range rates, and pre-war exercises had demonstrated that a skilled gunnery

Orion showing her two forward 13.5in gun turrets. Just aft of these is the heavily armoured conning tower from which the ship would fight and navigate in battle. The foremast is positioned aft of the smokestack, showing the obvious problems its occupants would encounter from smoke in many wind conditions.

officer provided better solutions. A much superior system, the Argo Clock, was available before the war, but was rejected. Eventually, the Argo system did find its way aboard a few dreadnoughts, and at least four ships were fitted with it at Jutland.

The Royal Navy used a system of centralized fire control, which relied on a central director, usually fitted in the foretop, that enabled all the ship's guns to be trained, laid and fired from a single position. The training angle and elevation for the guns were transmitted electronically from the director to each of the turrets, where the desired settings were laid automatically by the control systems in the turret.

The Germans did not develop such a sophisticated approach to fire control, a situation easily explained by the Germans' intention to fight at relatively short ranges. However, at Jutland, the German fire control system proved at least as effective as the British system. The Germans relied on 9ft 10in rangefinders, which like those of the British, were mounted on each turret and in the bridgework. In 1908, the Germans adopted a stereoscopic rangefinder and introduced a Dumaresq equivalent that provided target deflection. The German fire control system was very dependent on the skill of the artillery officer to estimate range rate. On German battleships, fire was controlled from the armoured conning tower, where the artillery officer took orders from the ship's commanding officer and spotted the fall of shot. The director-pointer system in the gunnery control tower generated a training angle for the turrets, but each turret was laid and fired individually.

PROTECTION

By 1905, the state-of-the-art battleship armour was Krupp cemented plate armour. At this time, normal battle ranges were assessed to be at 6,000 yards, and long-range engagements maybe out to 10,000 yards. At both these ranges, the shell of a high-velocity gun would strike its target's sides. For this reason, a dreadnought's armour was concentrated on its main belt on the hull. Weight penalties made it impossible to

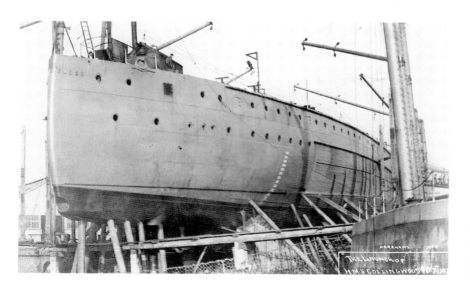

Collingwood under construction before her launch on November 1908. She was part of the third British class of dreadnoughts, but offered little improvement over Dreadnought. This view shows her stern torpedo tube. Both the British and Germans thought that battleship-launched torpedoes would be potent weapons in a dreadnought duel, and both retained them throughout the war. In practice, they proved utterly ineffective. Also note the recess in the hull where the belt armour would be fitted.

extend the main belt over the ship's entire length or up the entire height of the hull, so it was situated along the waterline to guard the ship's vital areas. In practice, this distribution meant that it extended from the forward-most turret to the most aft turret, providing protection for the magazines and propulsion spaces. The armour above the main belt was tapered and was primarily intended to provide protection against high-explosive shells – the effect of these shells against unarmoured parts of the ship was shown to be devastating in the Russo-Japanese war of 1904–05.

Both British and German battleships were well protected from heavy shell impacts at what was considered normal battle ranges, but as a matter of course German main belts were thicker than British ones. Since it was believed that heavy shells would not have the trajectory to strike the ship's horizontal areas, deck armour was comparatively light, sufficient to provide protection against splinter damage from shells bursting above. Later, when better fire control allowed for greater engagement ranges (10,000 yards and beyond), the trajectory of shells was steeper, which meant that it was the decks of the ships being struck, not the sides. Both British and German ships lacked adequate deck armour against heavy shells.

The advent of reliable torpedoes and the threat of mines demanded that early dreadnought designs provide adequate protection below the waterline. For the true vulnerability of early dreadnoughts was not against shellfire, but against underwater damage. This was especially true with British dreadnoughts, which lacked adequate protection from torpedoes, a fact that helped shape British tactics at Jutland. *Dreadnought* was designed with only a thin protective screen covering her magazines and shell rooms. The first German dreadnoughts, in contrast, were fitted with a continuous 1.25in anti-torpedo bulkhead that protected all her vital below-deck spaces. In their second class of dreadnought, the British enhanced underwater protection by extending the screen over all vital spaces in a comparable manner to the Germans. Yet from the Colossus to Iron Duke classes, the British reverted to the use of screens covering only the magazine spaces. The Queen Elizabeth and Revenge classes were fitted with anti-torpedo bulges, which were designed to detonate the torpedo as far as possible from the ship's internal bulkheads while also providing protection from splinter damage. The provision of a bulge, when properly designed, provided a high level of protection against the small torpedo warheads of the day, and was the equal of German underwater protection. Both the Royal Navy and the German Navy also attempted to provide underwater protection with elaborate subdivision schemes. In this area the Germans were more successful, since their ships had wider beams and closer subdivision requirements. Even subdivision, however, had its limits, as the pumping and drainage systems that passed though bulkheads still permitted the entry of floodwater when they were broken.

PROPULSION

Prior to *Dreadnought*, the main propulsion systems in battleships involved reciprocating machinery. The issue with reciprocating machinery was that it tended to overheat when run at high speeds over a sustained period, primarily because of difficulties with effective lubrication. Additionally, vibration at high speeds was a real problem. The steam turbine offered many potential advantages (see below), but in 1905 it remained an unproven technology, only being first used on a ship in 1897. The Royal Navy's decision to use turbines on *Dreadnought* was a bold one.

The introduction of turbines offered considerable weight advantages. For example, on *Dreadnought* the weight savings amounted to some 1,000 tons directly and indirectly, weight that could be devoted to additional armour or guns. In service, the turbine proved more reliable than reciprocating machinery and gave the ship the ability to steam at higher speeds for longer distances. Yet early turbines had problems due to the different rotational speed requirements of the turbines and the propellers. Turbines work most efficiently at higher rotational speeds contrasted to propellers that work better at lower rotational speeds. When the turbines were attached to the propellers by direct drive, this resulted in lower top speeds and increased fuel consumption. The introduction of geared turbines solved these problems, but this solution was not used on dreadnoughts until after the war. Another problem was apparent only after the start of the war, when dreadnoughts were more frequently run at high speeds. Such usage caused the brass seawater pipes in the condenser to leak, thus allowing saltwater into the feed water. This effect was known as 'impingement' and remained a problem throughout the war – during the first part of the war, dreadnoughts of both sides were placed out of action by this mechanical failure. In contrast to British ships, German ships used small-tube boilers and lighter materials. The extra space and weight savings could be devoted to extra protection, but British turbines and large-tube boilers proved to be very reliable in service.

During the war, the design of later dreadnoughts featured the use of oil fuel in preference to coal. The advantages of oil were obvious. When burned fully, oil provides 30 per cent more heat per pound than coal. Operationally, the use of oil suspended the need to re-coal every few days, a messy procedure. Refuelling with oil, by comparison, was much faster and easier. Beginning with the Queen Elizabeth class, all British dreadnoughts were oil-fired. The Germans did not introduce their first oil-fired dreadnought until the Bayern class.

When launched on 10 February 1906, *Dreadnought* revolutionized naval warfare. There were several weaknesses to her design, but her overall capabilities made previous battleships obsolete.

Temeraire pictured before the war. Built to a modified Dreadnought design, she still employed an awkward main battery layout, using wing turrets. Present at Jutland, she played only a minor part. She was later sent to Turkish waters in 1918, before being scrapped in 1922 after a brief period as a cadet ship.

ROYAL NAVY DREADNOUGHT DESIGNS

In general, it is accurate to say that the Royal Navy placed more importance on re-building a commanding numerical lead over its nearest dreadnought competitor than on producing ships of great quality. When compared with German dreadnoughts, British ships did not compare well individually, but any qualitative advantage the Germans may have possessed was overshadowed by the productivity of British shipyards.

Hercules pictured before the war. The booms located along the hull are for torpedo nets, but were removed in 1915–16. *Hercules* was the first attempt to break away from the basic Dreadnought design by abandoning the use of wing turrets in favour of an arrangement where all five turrets could fire broadside. This layout proved a failure in service. *Hercules* survived the war to go into reserve in 1919 and was scrapped in 1922.

Following the completion of *Dreadnought* in October 1906, the ship ran trials for another six months. Her design, and her unproven steam turbines, proved to be a complete success. Now the Royal Navy quickly had to build a lead in dreadnought numbers. Fisher included plans for four sister ships for *Dreadnought* in the 1906 budget, but only three were approved. These ships, known as the Bellerophon class, had less main belt armour than *Dreadnought*, but had better subdivision. In addition, the more effective 4in gun replaced the 3in gun as the ships' secondary battery. The Admiralty again asked for four dreadnoughts in 1907, but once more only three were approved. These became the St Vincent class, but they were essentially repeats of the *Dreadnought* design. The only significant difference was the provision of a new development of the 12in gun with better performance.

The fourth ship requested in 1907 was actually postponed to 1908 and was completed to a modified design. This ship, *Neptune*, featured a new layout for its ten 12in guns, designed to improve the broadside firepower. Instead of the wing turrets on *Dreadnought*, *Neptune* was fitted with the two middle turrets in a staggered arrangement that permitted each to fire crossdeck in a broadside. *Neptune* also featured the first use of superfiring turrets. The two additional dreadnoughts approved in 1909 were built to a similar design to *Neptune* and featured the use of the staggered or 'echelon' turret arrangement amidships. In service, however, this design was not practical and was not repeated. These ships also carried a heavier main armour belt, but underwater protection was inferior because of the deletion of torpedo bulkheads. Also approved in 1909 was the first of the 'super-dreadnoughts', so called because of the move up to a 13·5in gun. *Orion* was the first ship to carry the new weapon. Also for the first time, all five main battery turrets were mounted on the centre line, thus ensuring maximum broadside firepower.

In 1909, the naval race between Britain and Germany was in full swing. After the British government learned of the provisions of the German Supplementary Naval Law of 1908, the usual pace of three dreadnoughts per year was abandoned in favour of six battleships and four battlecruisers. The other three battleships approved in 1909 were also built to the *Orion* design, and were laid down in 1910. The next two classes,

Thunderer was the last ship laid down of the Orion class of super-dreadnoughts. Note that all her 13.5in turrets are located on the centreline with clear arcs of fire. At Jutland, she fired only 37 main gun rounds. After the war, she served as a cadet ship from 1921 to 1926, before being broken up.

IRON DUKE

The Iron Duke class was the most advanced of the Royal Navy's 13.5in gunned dreadnoughts. The lead ship of the class served as Jellicoe's flagship at Jutland, where she was undamaged. *Iron Duke* survived the Great War to become a gunnery training ship in 1932. She served in World War II and was not scrapped until 1946.

totalling eight ships, were little modified from the design of *Orion*. Four ships of the King George V class were approved in 1910 followed by four ships of the Iron Duke class in 1911. The Iron Dukes were fitted with the larger 6in-gun secondary battery made essential by the increasing size of torpedo boats and destroyers.

The next big step in Royal Navy dreadnought design was already in the works. Approval for the Queen Elizabeth class was given in 1912, and by 1913 work was begun on all five units. All were commissioned after the start of the war, yet all but one were present at Jutland. When launched they were beyond question the most powerful ships in the world. They were the first British dreadnoughts to move to an oil-fired propulsion system, and with their more powerful machinery they were the fastest battleships of the day. Armour was also increased. Most importantly, the new 15in gun was fitted; because the weight of shell was so much greater than the 13.5in gun, her designers were able to move to an eight-gun battery instead of the customary ten guns.

The last class of British battleships completed during the war were the five units of the Revenge class. These were planned to be heavily armed and armoured 21-knot ships suitable for work in the North Sea. As such, they were essentially a 15in gun version of the Iron Duke class. This intent, however, was thrown into confusion when Fisher returned as First Sea Lord in October 1914. He stopped the construction of the class and decided to fit oil-fired boilers to all five ships for a maximum speed of 23 knots. The ships were never able to achieve this speed, but essentially became slower versions of the Queen Elizabeth class. Three of the five ships were fitted with anti-torpedo bulges and it was found that the provision of these 6ft bulges reduced top speed by only less than half a knot.

Finally, in August 1914, four dreadnoughts were under construction in British yards for foreign navies. Two were earmarked for the Turkish Navy and were already

Queen Elizabeth was the epitome of British dreadnought design during the war. Of the five ships in the class, only *Queen Elizabeth* missed Jutland. All five were modernized to serve in World War II.

complete. These were quickly impounded and renamed *Erin* and *Agincourt* in British service. Chile had also ordered two ships and one was almost complete. As British relations with Chile were much better than with Turkey, these two Chilean ships were purchased in September 1914. The lead ship entered Royal Navy service in October and was named *Canada*. The second was completed in 1918 as an aircraft carrier.

GERMAN DREADNOUGHT DESIGN

From the very start, the Germans employed different dreadnought design principles from the British. German naval designers considered that protection was most important and the main German naval architect placed emphasis on an extensive system of underwater protection by dividing the ship's hull into a large number of narrow, watertight compartments. This configuration was made possible by a large beam, which also provided a very stable gun platform. The Germans usually devoted a larger proportion of a ship's displacement to armour, allowing for thicker main belts and for more of the ship to be given some degree of protection.

Conversely, German ships were usually less well armed than their British counterparts, partly due to weight considerations, which precluded the selection of large main guns on a design already devoting considerable weight to armour protection. Another reason was the German assessment that since the main battle area for their dreadnoughts was the North Sea, where poor visibility was the norm, guns larger than 12in were unnecessary. Thus, after the first class of dreadnought was fitted with 11in guns, the Germans settled on the 12in gun for all remaining classes, until finally adapting the 15in gun for their last class built during the war. The German 12in gun was clearly the equal to the early British 12in guns, but the Germans failed to respond in a timely manner as the British opened the firepower gap by adopting the 13.5in and finally the 15in guns.

Deutschland was the lead ship in the final class of German pre-dreadnoughts. Though their top speed was only 18 knots, Scheer decided to include the entire class with the High Seas Fleet in the Jutland operation. The weak underwater protection of the class was amply demonstrated when *Pommern* was blown up by a single torpedo hit, with the loss of her entire crew.

The Germans were also slow to adopt the steam turbine. Because of manufacturing difficulties and their unfamiliarity with the steam turbine, the first two classes of German dreadnoughts retained reciprocating machinery. Not until 1909 were new German dreadnoughts fitted with turbines, but once in service such ships were easily able to meet their design speeds. Before the war, the Germans explored the possibility of fitting a 2-stroke 12,000hp diesel engine to drive the central shaft and thereby increase cruising range, but after being tested on a single dreadnought this development was not pursued further. In general, since German battleships were expected to operate only in the North Sea, endurance was not a design emphasis. Habitability was also not emphasized, since ships would not be deployed for long periods and crews lived in barracks ashore when the ship was in port.

The first German dreadnoughts were the four ships of the Nassau class, which were designed in 1906 by improving the last of the pre-dreadnought designs. Because of problems with lengthening shipyard slipways to build the larger ships, construction did not begin until 1907. Compared with *Dreadnought*, the first German dreadnoughts possessed greater protection, but were armed with smaller guns (11in compared with 12in) and were slower.

The next four ships were authorized in the 1908–09 budget, and were all laid down in 1908. The four ships of the Helgoland class were slightly improved versions of the *Nassau* with armour protection being increased and a larger 12in gun fitted. However, the main battery layout still employed the use of wing turrets arranged in a manner that only eight of the 12 guns could be brought to bear broadside. This class also retained reciprocating steam engines, meaning that it was still slower than British dreadnoughts.

Kaiser, the lead ship of the next class, was laid down in 1909 with the remaining four ships of the class laid down in 1910. These were the first German dreadnoughts

Nassau was the first German dreadnought to enter service, in October 1909. This starboard view shows the ship's basic layout. Designed hurriedly as a counter to *Dreadnought*, she mounted two more main guns and was slightly better protected.

ABOVE
The four units of the Helgoland class continued the German emphasis on protection over firepower, though this class did introduce the 12in gun, which was superior to its British counterpart.

BELOW
A König class unit in the period before Jutland. This class was the first German dreadnought to place all main battery turrets on the centre line.

to use steam turbines, and all five ships of the class, including one fitted with an experimental diesel engine on one shaft, exceeded their design speed of 21 knots. Armour protection was again improved until total armour reached 40 per cent of the ship's normal displacement. The main battery was reduced to ten 12in guns in five turrets, but the two middle turrets were arranged in echelon to allow them to fire broadside in either direction. This layout, theoretically, increased the broadside to ten guns, but in practice it was not a success and it was not used again.

The last dreadnoughts laid down before the war were the four ships of the König class. The first three ships were authorized as part of the 1911–12 budget, and the last ship in the 1912–13 budget. All were completed in 1914 and all saw action at Jutland. They possessed the same superior level of protection found on the Kaiser class. The main difference was the placement of all five turrets on the ship's centre line.

KÖNIG

König shown in 1916 during the battle of Jutland. *König* was heavily damaged at Jutland, taking ten large-calibre British shells, the most of any German battleship present. She was never in any danger of sinking, but did suffer 45 dead and 27 wounded.

THE STRATEGIC SITUATION

With both fleets determined to accept action only under favourable circumstances, the opening of the war did not bring the major fleet engagement expected by many on both sides. The Grand Fleet conducted regular sweeps into the North Sea, but in the absence of opposition from the High Seas Fleet, the main enemies of British dreadnoughts became mines and submarines instead of German dreadnoughts.

The first action between British and German naval forces did not occur until 28 August, when the Royal Navy made plans to attack the German patrollers off Heligoland. In an action conducted in fog and haze, the Germans were initially surprised. The commander of the Grand Fleet's Battle Cruiser Force, Vice-Admiral Sir David Beatty bravely rushed into the fight in the face of a mine and torpedo threat in bad weather. The final result was the first British naval victory of the war, with three German light cruisers sunk. The larger effect was to make the Germans even more cautious, and the Kaiser went as far as ordering that the commander of the High Seas Fleet gain his personal approval before committing to an operation that might result in a fleet engagement.

Despite the Germans' reluctance to commit the High Seas Fleet to action, they increased submarine and minelaying operations. These paid dividends when on 5 September a U-boat sank a British scout cruiser, and on 22 September the old submarine *U-9* sank three armoured cruisers in succession off the Dutch coast, with a total loss of more than 1,400 men. The power of the submarine was now fully evident to the Royal Navy. Furthermore, on 27 October the dreadnought *Audacious*, out on firing practice, hit a mine off the coast of northern Ireland. The ship sank, more due to poor damage control than any design flaw.

The inactivity of the High Seas Fleet did not sit well with many, amongst them Tirpitz. He pressed for offensive operations. Though the commander of the High Seas Fleet, Admiral Friedrich von Ingenohl, declined to commit his ships to combat, for reasons of morale, some offensive action was desired. Accordingly, the High Seas Fleet's Scouting Force of battlecruisers and light cruisers under Rear Admiral Franz Hipper conducted a bombardment of Yarmouth on the east coast of England on 3 November.

Throughout the early part of the naval war in the North Sea, the British had the benefit of a high level of insight into German naval operations. The intelligence was provided by Room 40, the Royal Navy's code-breaking organization, named after its residence on the first floor of the old Admiralty Building. After an uncertain start, but bolstered by intelligence windfalls (including obtaining the current signal book from a German light cruiser that ran aground in the Baltic), Room 40 was invariably able to provide the Admiralty with advance warning of all pending major German naval operations. Room 40 did not always know the object of a German naval sortie, but it did develop reliable means to predict when the High Seas Fleet was at sea, often allowing the Grand Fleet to leave port before a German operation had even begun.

The Germans planned another bombardment raid on the English coast, this time against Scarborough and Hartlepool. On this occasion, Hipper's battlecruisers were supported by the High Seas Fleet itself, which came out as far as the Dogger Bank, about halfway across the North Sea. Room 40 was able to provide warning that another raid was imminent. In response, the Admiralty ordered Beatty's battlecruisers to a point where they could intercept the Germans on their way home. Jellicoe wanted to support the operation with the entire Grand Fleet, but was refused by the Admiralty, who thought that the 2nd Battle Squadron with six dreadnoughts was sufficient. The decision was a recipe for potential disaster, as Room 40 had not been

Audacious shown sinking on 27 October 1914, the first British dreadnought loss of the war. The loss of this vessel to a small mine was very unsettling to the Royal Navy. Her sinking was due more to the immature state of damage control in the Royal Navy at the time, rather than any design weakness.

29

Elements of the 4th Battle Squadron in a line-abreast formation in the North Sea in 1915. The nearest ship is an Iron Duke class ship, the second ship is *Agincourt* and the third is a ship of the Bellerophon class.

able to discern that the entire High Seas Fleet was also at sea and that they would be operating close by the six British dreadnoughts. It looked as if the Germans would get to engage a portion of the Grand Fleet with overwhelming force.

The events of the German raid on 16 December ended up being indecisive due to poor weather and command problems. The German warships conducted their bombardment and successfully avoided interception by Beatty's battlecruisers despite being spotted by Beatty's light cruiser scouts and later by elements of the 2nd Battle Squadron. Before the escape of the German battlecruisers, the High Seas Fleet had come into contact with the destroyer screen of the 2nd Battle Squadron. Instead of pressing the attack with his 14 dreadnoughts and eight pre-dreadnoughts, Ingenohl turned away when only 10 miles from the British force, fearful that he had come across the entire Grand Fleet and knowing he did not have the Kaiser's permission to engage in such a battle.

In January 1915, the Germans planned another raid into the Dogger Bank area to clear out fishing trawlers suspected of acting as British surveillance units, and to engage British light forces thought to be in the area. Hipper wanted support from the High Seas Fleet, but Ingenohl could not gain the Kaiser's permission to sail the fleet that far into the North Sea. Unfortunately for the Germans, Room 40 had deciphered orders for the operation and the British had prepared an ambush. On 24 January 1915, the three battlecruisers and one armoured cruiser under Hipper were spotted and were soon being pursued by Beatty's five battlecruisers. In a confused action marked by British signalling problems, the five British battlecruisers were able to sink only the armoured cruiser *Blücher*, while allowing the three battlecruisers to escape.

The battle of Dogger Bank had severe repercussions for the Germans. Ingenohl was replaced by Admiral Hugo von Pohl and the Kaiser instructed von Pohl that he could not seek battle beyond the minefields of the Heligoland Bight. Most importantly, it was obvious that the German strategy of attrition in the North Sea was not working. In order to hurt the British, another method had to be found. The only alternative was to utilize submarines. On 4 February 1915, the Germans declared the waters around Britain and Ireland a military zone in which merchant ships were liable for destruction.

The first unrestricted submarine campaign ran from February to October 1915. The Germans lacked sufficient submarines to make a blockade effective, but early results were encouraging and British anti-submarine efforts were inadequate. The real problem for the Germans was dealing with the diplomatic fallout of attacking neutral shipping, particularly that of the United States. In this environment, an incident involving American ships or American casualties was inevitable, and it came on 7 May 1915, when a German submarine sank the Cunard liner *Lusitania* with the loss of 1,201 lives, 128 of them American. The Germans avoided an American entry into the war with some concessions to their submarine blockade, but by September submarine attacks had reverted to the restrictive prize rules. The first unrestricted submarine campaign had failed, but the potential of the submarine had been fully demonstrated while the High Seas Fleet sat idly in port.

Following the failure of the unrestricted submarine campaign, events moved in a direction that would finally result in a clash at sea between the great dreadnought fleets. The first of these was the death of Pohl in February 1916 from cancer. His replacement was Vice Admiral Reinhard Scheer, who was much more offensively minded. He was also an advocate of a renewed submarine campaign. The Kaiser, however, could not bring himself to approve another round of unrestricted submarine warfare until some type of understanding had been reached with the Americans. What resulted was a restricted U-boat offensive that quickly ran into diplomatic troubles.

Complementing the U-boat campaign was a number of other measures intended to put constant pressure on the British and force them to take actions that might bring the Germans the opportunity of an engagement on favourable terms. Amongst these

In one of the most iconic maritime photos of all time, German armoured cruiser *Blücher* is shown capsizing on 24 January 1915, during the battle of Dogger Bank. This battle marked the end of a series of German raids on the English coast during the early part of the war. It was not until Jutland that the opposing battlecruiser forces would meet again.

measures were intensified sweeps by the High Seas Fleet, including the renewed bombardment of British coastal towns. The first of Scheer's fleet movements occurred on 5–6 March 1916, when he sortied to a point south of Dogger Bank to intercept British light units on patrol. Though the Grand Fleet tried to intercept, there was no action. On 25 March, the British mounted an operation to launch an aircraft raid from a seaplane carrier against German Zeppelin stations on the Schleswig coast. The five aircraft that were launched inflicted no damage, but did prompt the High Seas Fleet to put to sea. The seaplane carrier was being covered by Beatty's Battle Cruiser Force, but was ordered to withdraw when the German sortie was discovered. The Grand Fleet was ordered to a position off the Scottish coast, but bad weather prevented the Germans from advancing farther into the North Sea and both sides returned to base.

Jellicoe resisted mounting pressure from the Admiralty to be more aggressive. The Admiralty supported the notion that further air raids would force the Germans out to fight. Jellicoe did not think this outcome was as likely, and worried that even if the Germans did emerge it would be late in the day before they would be in a position clear of the minefields, leaving insufficient time for the Grand Fleet to engage them decisively. Jellicoe also worried about the fuel consumption of his destroyers and light cruisers, which would prevent him from lingering long off the German coast waiting for the High Seas Fleet to emerge. In Jellicoe's mind, he was unable to force the Germans out, so any engagement would result from a German attempt to seize the initiative.

On 20 April, the British mounted an operation into the Kattegat to attack German shipping. In response to intelligence that the High Seas Fleet was at sea, the Grand Fleet rushed to intercept, but were frustrated by heavy fog. Scheer took the initiative on 24 April, when he sortied his battlecruisers, supported by the High Seas Fleet, to conduct a bombardment of Lowestoft. The British, again advised by Room 40 that an operation was under way, sortied the Grand Fleet and the Battle Cruiser Fleet. The Germans battlecruisers encountered British light forces and then pressed on to shell Lowestoft, followed by Yarmouth. Declining an opportunity to press an attack on the British naval units, the battlecruisers, accompanied by the High Seas Fleet, headed west to their bases. The Grand Fleet, impeded by heavy seas, was not able to intercept.

In the series of raids and counter-raids, the next move was the Royal Navy's. On 4 May, two British seaplane carriers moved into position off the Schleswig coast to mount another attack on Zeppelin sheds. Only one of the 11 aircraft intended to take part in the raid actually bombed its target, but the sheds were not the real target. Jellicoe hoped that this action would entice the High Seas Fleet to sortie; in preparation the British had mined the German channels and moved submarines into the area. After lingering with the Grand Fleet, Jellicoe departed. By the time the Germans did come out later in the day, the British were gone.

Given the heightened activity by the German and British navies, it was becoming more likely that a clash between fleets would occur. But as both sides still sought to engage on favourable terms, any such clash would still be the result of accident. Jellicoe decided to keep the pressure up with a planned operation into the Kattegat with light forces on 2 June, supported by a battle squadron positioned in the Skaggerak and the entire Grand Fleet farther to the north-west. This operation was supported by submarines and a minelayer to attack the High Seas Fleet if it emerged. Concurrently, Scheer was making plans for a bombardment of Sunderland by his battlecruisers, to again attempt to draw out a portion of the Grand Fleet. The bombardment would be supported by the High Seas Fleet positioned south of the Dogger Bank. A force of 18 U-boats was stationed off British naval bases to attack British capital ships. German Navy Zeppelins would overwatch the entire operation to provide scouting reports and make sure the Grand Fleet was not intervening. Hipper would draw any intercepting British force onto the High Seas Fleet for it to deliver a crushing blow. Yet because of maintenance issues with key units, Scheer had to push the planned operation back to the end of May. Poor weather prevented adequate Zeppelin coverage, and the endurance of the U-boats already stationed off British naval bases was reaching its limits. Scheer therefore decided to abandon the planned bombardment in favour of an operation targeted against British light units and shipping in the Skaggerak. The German battlecruiser force was ordered to show itself off the Norwegian coast to draw the British out.

At 0100hrs on 31 May 1916, the German battlecruisers left port, followed by the main body of the High Seas Fleet. As usual, Room 40 informed Jellicoe that something was up, and the Grand Fleet was already at sea when the Germans departed. The great clash was finally at hand.

Benbow, an Iron Duke class super-dreadnought, leading other ships of the 4th Battle Squadron in 1915. The potential for the smoke produced by a group of dreadnoughts to affect visibility is readily apparent.

TECHNICAL SPECIFICATIONS

BRITISH BATTLESHIPS

Following the successful trials of *Dreadnought*, the British moved quickly to build a numerical dreadnought superiority over any potential rival. The lead ship of the Bellerophon class was laid down in December 1906 and all three units were completed by May 1909. The Bellerophon vessels were a virtual repeat of *Dreadnought*. The main battery of ten 12in guns was mounted in five turrets, three placed on the centreline. The other two turrets were wing turrets, so that an eight-gun broadside was possible. The secondary armament was deficient, with only 16 4in guns, which were inadequate to stop a destroyer attack. In addition, the guns were badly placed, with eight being located on the top of the main turrets. By 1916, all 4in guns were moved to more workable positions in the superstructure.

On the heels of the Bellerophon class, the first ship of the St Vincent class was laid down in February 1907. The three ships of this class were essentially a repeat of the previous design, but did incorporate slight improvements. The layout of the main battery remained the same, but the main weapon was a more powerful version of the 12in gun. The 4in gun was retained as the secondary armament. Armour protection was largely the same as in the preceding class. The power of the machinery was increased to compensate for a slightly larger displacement. Combined with a more efficient longer hull, the class easily reached its design speed of 21 knots.

Not until the programme of 1909 did the Royal Navy attempt to depart from the basic design of *Dreadnought*. The three ships of the Neptune class attempted to address the principal flaw in the layout of the main battery of *Dreadnought*. Within the

Bellerophon class	
Ships in class	*Bellerophon*, *Superb*, *Temeraire*
Displacement (normal)	18,596 tons
Dimensions	length 526ft; beam 82ft 6in; draught 31ft
Armament	10 × 12in/45cal guns; 16 × 4in guns; 3 × 18in torpedo tubes
Protection	main belt 10−5in; deck 3−1.5in; turrets 12in; conning tower 11in; barbettes 10−5in; torpedo bulkhead 3−1in; weight of armour 5,430 tons (28.7 per cent of normal displacement)
Machinery	4-shaft Parsons turbines and 18 boilers creating 23,000hp; top speed 20.75 knots
Range	5,720 nautical miles (nm) at 10 knots
Crew	840 (1914)

Neptune class, there were significant modifications between the first ship of the class and the other two. Overall, the design proved unsatisfactory and was not repeated.

While several navies, principally the US Navy, had already moved to placing all main gun turrets on the centre line, the Royal Navy was reluctant to do so because of the design of its turrets. The problem was that the sighting hoods at the front of the turrets made the occupants inside susceptible to being concussed if a superimposed turret fired over them. Royal Navy designers still considered it essential that its battleships carry ten main guns and it was intended to enable all of these to fire broadside. *Neptune* introduced echeloned guns amidship, which in theory enabled all ten guns to be brought to bear broadside. This was the same layout explored on the first battlecruiser design, and as on *Invincible* it was found to be impractical in service due to the blast effect and strain on the hull when the guns were fired crossdeck. On top of this, the Number 4 turret was superimposed over the Number 5 turret, which

Superb pictured before the war. Before the start of the war, the height of her topmasts was reduced and the 4in guns removed from the top of the 12in main battery. *Superb* was present at Jutland, but played a minor role. In 1918, she was sent to Turkish waters as the flagship of British naval forces. After being used as a target ship in 1922, she was broken up in 1923.

Collingwood retained the inefficient wing-turret arrangements of early British dreadnoughts. Present at Jutland, she was undamaged, but barely missed being torpedoed. She went into reserve in 1919 and was scrapped in 1923.

meant that the Number 4 could not be fired astern. To clear the decks for crossdeck firing, the ship's boats were placed on a flying bridge between the smokestacks. This awkward arrangement was an obvious source of trouble in battle if damaged, so it was removed just after the outbreak of war. The same 12in/50 gun was used as on the St Vincent class, and armour protection was on a similar scale.

The later two ships of the class, *Colossus* and *Hercules*, were not laid down until July 1909 and were able to incorporate several modifications. The principal difference was in armour protection. As a weight-saving measure, the scale of protection on *Dreadnought* had been reduced on subsequent classes. Protection on *Colossus* and *Hercules* was improved to 11in on the main belt and the barbettes, returning protection to that of *Dreadnought*. The Royal Navy still believed that torpedoes were important weapons in a battleship duel, and now the longer-ranged 21in torpedo was introduced on battleships. The appearance of the later two ships was also altered. On previous British dreadnought designs, the placement of the smokestacks made the aft control position on the rear mast practically unusable due to smoke. The after mast

St Vincent class	
Ships in class	*Collingwood, St Vincent, Vanguard*
Displacement (normal)	19,700 tons
Dimensions	length 536ft; beam 84ft; draught 27–31ft
Armament	10 × 12in/50cal gun; 18 × 4in guns; 3 × 18in torpedo tubes
Protection	main belt 10–8in; deck 3–1.5in; turrets 11in; conning tower 11in; barbettes 9–5in; torpedo bulkhead 3–1.5in; weight of armour 5,590 tons (28 per cent of normal displacement)
Machinery	4-shaft Parsons turbines and 18 boilers creating 24,500hp; top speed 21 knots
Range	6,900nm at 10 knots
Crew	823 (1915)

Colossus pictured before the war. Her design was deficient in terms of turret and smokestack placement, and her protection showed no improvement over *Dreadnought* launched four years earlier. *Colossus* survived the war and served in various training capacities before being broken up in 1928.

was now dropped to save weight. At the same time, though, the forward smokestack was placed in front of the forward mast, introducing the same problems with smoke and making the ship's only remaining fire-control station virtually unusable.

In late 1909, the first ship of the four-ship Orion class was laid down. All four had entered service by 1912. These ships displayed the best British battleship design to date, and represented a significant increase in capabilities over previous designs. The principal difference was the decision to move to a 13.5in gun. The main battery was still ten guns, but for the first time all five turrets were mounted on the centre line, allowing for a ten-gun broadside. The decision to place superfiring turrets fore and aft

Neptune class	
Ships in class	*Neptune, Colossus, Hercules*
Displacement (normal)	19,680 tons (*Colossus* and *Hercules* 20,030 tons)
Dimensions	length 546ft; beam 85ft; draught 28ft 6in (*Colossus* and *Hercules* 29ft 5in)
Armament	10 × 12in/50cal guns; 16 × 4in guns; 3 × 21in torpedo tubes
Protection	main belt 10–2.5in (*Colossus* and *Hercules* 11–7in); deck 3–1.5in (*Colossus* and *Hercules* 4–1.5in); turrets 11in; conning tower 11in; barbettes 10–5in (*Colossus* and *Hercules* 11–4in); weight of armour (*Colossus* and *Hercules*) 5,562 tons (27.3 per cent of normal displacement)
Machinery	4-shaft Parsons turbines and 18 boilers creating 25,000hp; top speed 21 knots
Range	6,620nm at 10 knots (*Colossus* and *Hercules* 6,680nm)
Crew	813 (*Colossus* and *Hercules* 791 in 1916)

Orion class	
Ships in class	*Conqueror, Monarch, Orion, Thunderer*
Displacement (normal)	22,200 tons
Dimensions	length 581ft; beam 88ft 6in; draught 31ft 3in
Armament	10 × 13.5in/45cal guns; 16 × 4in guns; 3 × 18in torpedo tubes
Protection	main belt 12–8in; deck 4–1in; turrets 11in; conning tower 11in; barbettes 10–3in; weight of armour 6,560 tons (29 per cent of normal displacement)
Machinery	4-shaft Parsons turbines and 18 boilers creating 27,000hp; top speed 21 knots
Range	6,730nm at 10 knots
Crew	754 (1914)

included the restriction not to fire directly fore and aft, because of the concussion problem to personnel in the lower turret. Yet this arrangement was thought to be tactically insignificant compared with the advantage of being able to fire a full ten-gun broadside. In addition to the increase in firepower, protection was also increased on the main belt and the turret barbettes, giving the class a fine balance of offensive and defensive qualities. A continuing design flaw was the placement of the forward smokestack in front of the mainmast, which created problems with smoke in the fire-direction centre.

The four ships of the King George V class were all laid down in 1911 and had all entered service by 1913. These were essentially repeats of the Orions. The layout of the main battery was retained, but an improved model of the 13.5in gun was fitted, which fired a heavier shell. The secondary armament was still inadequate to deal with torpedo boats and destroyers, and the layout of the 16 4in guns was modified to

Dreadnought began the war as flagship of the 4th Battle Squadron, but in May 1916 she was temporarily transferred to the 3rd Battle Squadron when it was transferred from the Grand Fleet to Sheerness to boost defences against further German raids. As a result, *Dreadnought* missed Jutland.

King George V class

Ships in class	*Ajax, Audacious, Centurion, King George V*
Displacement (normal)	25,420 tons
Dimensions	length 597ft 6in; beam 89ft; draught 28ft 8in
Armament	10 × 13.5in/45cal guns; 16 × 4in guns; 3 × 21in torpedo tubes
Protection	main belt 12−8in; deck 4−1in; turrets 11in; conning tower 11in; barbettes 10−3in; weight of armour 7,080 tons (30.2 per cent of normal displacement)
Machinery	4-shaft Parsons turbines and 18 boilers creating 27,000hp; top speed 21 knots
Range	6,310nm at 10 knots
Crew	1,114 (1916)

include the fitting of four guns forward below the main deck level. It proved impossible to use these guns in any kind of sea, and all were removed during the war.

At the start of the Great War, two of the four ships of the Iron Duke class were already in service, with the other two due to commission before the end of the year. Thus, at the start of the war these were the most powerful battleships in the Royal Navy. The principal difference between these ships and those of the very similar Orion and King George V classes was the overdue provision of a secondary battery of 6in guns. Ten of the 12 guns, however, were placed in single casemates forward and close to the waterline, making them subject to interference from heavy seas and spray. The last two guns were mounted even lower in the area of the Number 5 turret. This placement proved so troublesome that the guns were removed and mounted in the forward superstructure before the battle of Jutland. These ships were the first Royal Navy battleships to mount anti-aircraft guns.

The five ships of the Queen Elizabeth class were the most successful of any British battleship design of World War I. Laid down in 1912−13, none were available by the start of the war, but all had been completed and were in service for the battle of Jutland. The lead ship of the class was in refit during Jutland, but the remaining four ships all saw action against the High Seas Fleet.

Iron Duke class

Ships in class	*Benbow, Emperor of India, Iron Duke, Marlborough*
Displacement (normal)	26,100 tons
Dimensions	length 623ft; beam 90ft; draught 32ft 9in
Armament	10 × 13.5in/45cal guns; 12 × 6in guns; 3 × 3in anti-aircraft guns; 4 × 21in torpedo tubes
Protection	main belt 12−8in; deck 2.5−1in; turrets 11in; conning tower 11in; barbettes 11in; weight of armour 7,925 tons (31.2 per cent of normal displacement)
Machinery	4-shaft Parsons turbines and 18 boilers creating 29,000hp; top speed 21 knots
Range	8,100nm at 12 knots
Crew	1,102 (1914)

The design incorporated several significant improvements. The most important of these was the decision to abandon the mixed coal and oil fuel system on previous British dreadnoughts in favour of an all-oil fuel system. This move was driven by the requirement to create a much higher output to meet the design speed of 25 knots with no extra weight in machinery. The decision to go to oil also saved enough weight that the scale of armour protection could actually be increased in some key areas. The result was a squadron of fast battleships with excellent protection. The Admiralty envisioned that the 'Fast Squadron' would be used to bring a reluctant enemy force to battle, and it possessed the speed to operate with the Grand Fleet's battlecruiser squadron.

The other major improvement on the Queen Elizabeth class was the decision to move up to a 15in gun. The larger gun was important for a number of reasons. The requirement to fit additional boilers to meet the 25-knot speed requirement meant that a turret amidships could not be fitted, but the British were reluctant to abandon the hitting power presented by a ten-gun battleship. If a 15in gun was fitted, however, the total broadside weight of an eight-gun 15in broadside would actually be greater than ten 13.5in guns.

A follow-up to the Queen Elizabeth class was the eight planned ships of the Revenge class. Of these, only five were completed, and of those only two (*Revenge* and *Royal Oak*) participated in Jutland. The Revenge class maintained the same scale of protection and the same 15in-gun main battery, but were not designed to have the same high speed.

Additionally, there were several battleships intended for foreign governments that the Royal Navy expropriated at the start of the war. All of these participated in the clash at Jutland. *Erin* was laid down in 1911 for Turkey, but was taken into British service in 1914. She gave the Royal Navy a unit possessing the same capabilities as an Iron Duke-class ship, with the same main and secondary armament and a similar scale of protection. *Agincourt* was originally ordered by Brazil, but was sold in January 1914, uncompleted, to Turkey. Along with *Erin,* she was destined never to fly the Turkish flag, being confiscated by the Royal Navy in 1914. *Agincourt* was not a well-balanced design. She did not possess the level of armour protection of other British

Queen Elizabeth class	
Ships in class	*Barham, Malaya, Queen Elizabeth, Valiant, Warspite*
Displacement (normal)	32,590 tons
Dimensions	length 639ft 9in (*Barham* and *Warspite* 643ft 9in); beam 90ft 7in; draught 33ft
Armament	8 × 15in/42cal guns; 14 × 6in guns; 4 × 21in torpedo tubes
Protection	main belt 13–8in; deck 3–1in; turrets 13in; conning tower 11in; barbettes 10–4in; weight of armour 8,900 tons (30 per cent of normal displacement)
Machinery	4-shaft Parsons turbines (Brown-Curtis in *Barham* and *Valiant*); 24 boilers creating 75,000hp; top speed 24 knots
Range	5,000nm at 12 knots
Crew	1,016 (1916)

Royal Sovereign class	
Ships in class	*Ramillies, Resolution, Revenge, Royal Oak, Royal Sovereign*
Displacement (full load)	29,590 tons (*Revenge*)
Dimensions	length 614ft 6in; beam 88ft 6in (without torpedo bulge); draught 30ft
Armament	8 × 15in/42cal guns; 14 × 6in guns; 2 × 3in anti-aircraft guns; 4 × 21in torpedo tubes
Protection	main belt 13in; deck 4–1in; turrets 13in; conning tower 11in; barbettes 10in; weight of armour 8,380 tons (29.4 per cent of normal displacement)
Machinery	4-shaft Parsons turbines with 18 boilers creating 40,000hp; top speed 23 knots (*Ramillies* 22 knots)
Range	7,000nm at 10 knots
Crew	909 (1916)

battleships, but compensated for this with enormous firepower. Her main battery was 14 14in guns (largest of any World War I dreadnought) mounted in seven centre line turrets, permitting all 14 guns to fire broadside. *Canada* was laid down in 1911 for Chile, and completed in late 1915. The Royal Navy purchased the ship and she proved to be a welcome addition to the Grand Fleet. The design was based on *Iron Duke*, but since the ship was longer and mounted more powerful machinery, her top speed was almost 23 knots. Armament was an impressive ten 14in guns (all centre line) and 18 6in guns. Her level of protection was not equal to the *Iron Duke*'s, but was similar to earlier British dreadnoughts. In service, she was considered one of the Grand Fleet's best ships.

GERMAN BATTLESHIPS

The German Navy was never able to maintain the Royal Navy's pace of dreadnought construction. There were fewer yards in Germany capable of building large ships. Those that could do so were much less efficient than their British counterparts, which could complete a dreadnought in a year. In contrast, German yards took typically from two to three years. By the opening of the war, and up until the time of Jutland, the German Navy was able to complete four classes of dreadnoughts for a total of 17 units. To compensate, the Germans augmented the High Seas Fleet with the most modern of their pre-dreadnoughts. In addition to the 17 dreadnoughts completed before Jutland, six battlecruisers were also in service. One of these, however, was caught in the Mediterranean at the war's beginning and by 1916 was nominally part of the Turkish Navy.

The Nassau class was the German Navy's response to *Dreadnought*. Caught unprepared, German naval designers took six months after the completion of *Dreadnought* to settle on the design, and the first ship of the class was not laid down until June 1907. The four ships of the class were completed between October 1909 and May 1910, each having taken between two and three years to complete.

The design of this first German dreadnought set the pattern for future construction. Yet the Germans were forced to use the triple-expansion machinery from their pre-dreadnought designs, as there was no time to develop turbines without suffering an even greater delay. With improved horsepower from earlier designs, the ships could just make 20 knots. In 1915, all four ships in the class were modified to burn fuel oil which was sprayed on the coal.

The strength of the class was its protection, particularly below the waterline. The main battery was mounted in six turrets, each with two 11in guns. The layout of these turrets allowed for only two on the centre line, with the other four placed two on each side of the ship, making the broadside only eight guns firing a comparatively light shell weight of 6,080lb. The secondary battery comprised 12 5.9in guns, arranged in single casemates six per side.

With the naval race with the Royal Navy heating up, the Germans laid down four ships of the Helgoland class in 1908. Because speed was of the essence, this class was based on the Nassau class with only minor improvements. The biggest change was the shift to a 12in gun in an attempt to match the Royal Navy's advantage in broadside shell weight. The layout of the main battery was a repeat of the Nassau class, so that only eight guns could be brought to bear broadside. The secondary battery comprised 14 single 5.9in guns mounted in casemates.

Nassau class	
Ships in class	*Rheinland, Posen, Nassau, Westfalen*
Displacement (normal)	18,900 tons
Dimensions	length 478ft; beam 89ft; draught 27ft 6in
Armament	12 × 11in/45cal guns; 12 × 5.9in/45cal guns; 16 × 3.4in guns; 6 × 17.7in torpedo tubes
Protection	main belt 11.5–4in; deck 4in; turrets 11in; conning tower 12in; weight of armour 6,640 tons (35.2 per cent of normal displacement)
Machinery	3-shaft vertical triple-expansion and 12 boilers creating 22,000hp; top speed 19.5 knots
Range	9,400nm at 10 knots
Crew	1,130 (wartime)

Because of the requirement to begin construction as soon as possible, the authorities again decided not to wait for turbines. Speed was increased incrementally by the provision of greater power and a longer hull. A wider beam was provided, and this was used to provide a better internal arrangement. The magazines for the wing 12in turrets were provided with improved underwater protection and were less crowded. All of the boilers were also grouped together, which allowed the ship's three smokestacks to be placed together amidships.

The next class of dreadnoughts was laid down in 1910. This class, named for the Kaiser, included several important developments. The Germans had successfully incorporated turbines into their battlecruisers, and now they were fitted on a class of dreadnoughts. The 12in gun was retained, but the layout of the main battery was revised. Three of the five turrets were fitted on the centre line (one forward and two aft), and the remaining two were fitted amidships in a staggered arrangement that theoretically allowed both turrets to fire broadside. In reality, this arrangement proved impractical. The amidships turrets were too close to the fore and aft superstructures to permit them to fire fore and aft without creating blast damage. Crossdeck fire on the broadside was also difficult, as it placed great stresses on the hull.

Posen shown after the start of the war, essentially unchanged apart from the removal of some of her prominent radio gaffs. She fired 53 11in rounds at Jutland and was undamaged. After the war, she was handed over to Great Britain and scrapped in 1921.

Helgoland class	
Ships in class	*Ostfriesland, Thuringen, Helgoland, Oldenburg*
Displacement (normal)	22,800 tons
Dimensions	length 546ft; beam 93ft 6in; draught 27ft 6in
Armament	12 × 12in/50cal guns; 14 × 5.9in/45cal guns; 14 (reduced to 12 in 1913) × 3.4in guns; 6 × 19.7in torpedo tubes
Protection	main belt 11.75–4in; deck 3in; turrets 11in; conning tower 12in; weight of armour 8,350 tons (36.6 per cent of normal displacement)
Machinery	3-shaft vertical triple-expansion and 15 boilers creating 28,000hp; top speed 20 knots
Range	9,400nm at 10 knots
Crew	1,300 (wartime)

Protection was increased over previous dreadnought classes, and was superior to comparable British classes. The ships developed more than their designed power, in the case of *Kaiser* up to 55,000hp, so were able to make up to 23.4 knots. *Friedrich der Grosse* was selected in 1914 to be refitted as the fleet flagship and was fitted with a heavy foremast which gave her a different appearance from her sister ships.

The four ships of the König class were laid down in 1911 and at the time of Jutland were the most modern dreadnoughts in the High Seas Fleet. The class retained ten 12in guns as its main armament, which were mounted in five turrets. However, the awkward arrangement of the two amidships turrets from the Kaiser class was altered in favour of all turrets being fitted on the centre line. The centre line turret between the stacks gave these ships a ten-gun broadside, the first ever for a German dreadnought. The secondary armament remained at 14 5.9in guns, each mounted singly in casemates.

With an increased beam, a high level of subdivision was again in evidence. As in the Kaiser class, the boiler rooms and machinery were grouped fore and aft of the amidships turret, which created the widely spaced smokestacks. Unlike previous classes, a heavy tubular foremast was fitted with a control top.

Kaiser class

Ships in class	*Friedrich der Grosse, Kaiserin, König Albert, Prinzregent Luitpold, Kaiser*
Displacement (normal)	24,720 tons
Dimensions	length 564ft; beam 95ft 3in; draught 27ft 3in
Armament	10 × 12in/50cal guns; 14 × 5.9in/45cal guns; 12 (reduced to 10 by 1915) × 3.4in guns; 5 × 19.7in torpedo tubes
Protection	main belt 13.75–7.75in; deck 3in; turrets 11.75in; conning tower 13.75in; weight of armour 10,100 tons (40.1 per cent of normal displacement)
Machinery	3-shaft Parsons turbines and 16 boilers creating 31,000hp; top speed 21 knots. *Prinzregent Luitpold* equipped with 2-shaft Parsons turbines and 14 boilers creating 26,000hp; top speed 20 knots.
Range	9,500nm at 10 knots
Crew	1,250 (wartime)

König class

Ships in class	*König*, *Grosser Kurfürst*, *Markgraf* and *Kronprinz*
Displacement (normal)	25,800 tons
Dimensions	length 580ft; beam 97ft; draught 28ft 6in
Armament	10 × 12in/50cal guns; 14 × 5.9in/45cal guns; 6 × 3.4in guns; 2 × 3.4 in anti-aircraft guns; 5 × 19.7in torpedo tubes
Protection	main belt 14–10in; deck 4.5in; turrets 14in; conning tower 14in; weight of armour 10,440 tons (40.4 per cent of normal displacement)
Machinery	3-shaft Parsons turbines and 12 boilers creating 31,000hp; top speed 21 knots
Range	10,000nm at 10 knots
Crew	1,300 (wartime)

Prinzregent Luitpold photographed immediately before the outbreak of war. As a member of the Kaiser class, she continued the trend of emphasizing protection over firepower, but was a more effective fighting unit than her British contemporaries. Undamaged at Jutland, she was scuttled at Scapa Flow in June 1919.

The König class comprised the elite V Division of III Squadron. All fought at Jutland and after the war all were surrendered in November 1918, and scuttled in June 1919.

THE COMBATANTS

ROYAL NAVY DREADNOUGHT CREWS

The Royal Navy went to war with a foundation of highly trained and motivated crews for its dreadnoughts. All personnel were volunteers, and, in addition to being committed to long service careers, the same personnel were assigned to a single ship for extended periods, making for cohesive crews.

For generations, entry into the Royal Navy as an officer was based far more on class status and the ability of the applicant's parents to support the prospective officer, rather than raw talent. In 1916, almost all of a British dreadnought's officers would have come through the Britannia Royal Naval College. An applicant typically joined at 13 and was sent to college for four years, followed by six months on a training cruiser. At that point, the aspirant joined the fleet as a midshipman. When commissioned, almost all new officers selected navigation and gunnery career paths; engineering was not viewed as a suitable career for a gentleman.

Promotion from the lower deck was very rare and a point of contention until 1912, when First Lord of the Admiralty Winston Churchill devised the Mate Scheme, whereby petty officers and above could attain commissioned status with the rank of mate (equivalent to lieutenant). The option was later extended to engineers in 1914. In 1913, Churchill introduced a special entry scheme whereby cadets from public schools could join the Royal Navy at 18, take two cruises, and then be sent to the fleet as midshipmen. This measure did much to provide the Royal Navy with most of its engineers.

There was strict segregation between the upper deck (officers) and the lower deck (ratings). The bulk of a dreadnought's crew was composed of enlisted personnel. Young working-class men were drawn to the Royal Navy for security and adventure. Despite the long hours and severe discipline, working conditions in the Navy compared favourably with his other career options. Before the outbreak of the war, the Royal Navy was able to take its pick of available applicants. Those that were accepted could join as early as 15 or 16 years old, and committed themselves to a 12-year hitch. Training began with a six-week stint of seamanship and basic schooling, followed by specialized training.

Life aboard a capital ship was crowded, given the large size of a dreadnought crew. The lower deck was divided into a separate mess for each division or specialization. When not on watch or performing their specific tasks, ratings had to eat, sleep and spend off-duty time in the same crowded space. Meals were collected from the galley and brought to the messing area. Food was plentiful but generally unimaginative, since refrigerated storage was not available. Once the meal was finished, the same area was used for sleeping, with ratings accommodated in hammocks. One of the traditional benefits was a daily rum ration, usually served at lunch.

Life on a British dreadnought was more about monotony than anything else. Because the base at Scapa Flow was not developed at

Admiral Sir David Beatty shown in 1918 with King George V after Beatty assumed command of the Grand Fleet. His performance at Jutland was marked by over-aggressiveness and a series of command and control difficulties. His Battle Cruiser Fleet came off second best to Hipper's battlecruisers.

the start of the war, and was not judged to be safe from U-boat attack, the Grand Fleet spent the first few months of the war continually at sea. When not at sea, the crew was coaling or replenishing stores. Even when Scapa Flow was finished in 1915, it offered a cold and dreary alternative to life at sea, with very limited distractions ashore. Most men remained on the ship, spending the time engaged in sports, movies or education. Jellicoe designed an extensive programme of fleet exercises to counteract the boredom. The Grand Fleet went to sea often for training. While inside Scapa Flow, there was adequate space for daily (except Sunday) gunnery and torpedo drills. Gunnery exercises were conducted at regular intervals to the west of Pentland Firth, and involved a squadron of dreadnoughts engaging towed targets. Even in the bays of Scapa Flow, ships would shoot at targets towed by picket boats. Ships would also engage in gunnery practice at night, with searchlights providing illumination.

What is hard to quantify is the Royal Navy's psychological edge created by the Royal Navy's tradition of victory and dominance. The upstart German Navy went into the battle with an inferiority complex. In the words of Scheer himself: 'The English Fleet has the advantage of looking back on a hundred years of proud tradition which must have given every man a sense of superiority based on the great deeds of the past.'

GERMAN BATTLESHIP CREWS

In 1897, the entire German Navy had only 1,000 officers and a total personnel strength of about 26,000. By 1914, personnel strength had swollen to 80,000, including 3,612 officers. In order to support the increasing complexity of the Kaiser's navy, many technical skills were required, hence there were several branches of the officer corps – marine infantry, engineer, torpedo engineer, ordnance, ordnance artificer, torpedo and medical. The premier branch, however, was the executive branch, as only its personnel were entitled to command a ship.

The German Navy's officers were drawn to naval service for a number of reasons, including a sense of adventure, desire for travel and not least the desire for social prestige and quick promotion (at least compared with the army). Each year, about 200 candidates were accepted as officers, a fraction of those who applied. The cost of training put a career as a naval officer out of reach of the lower strata of society. Criteria for selection was at the discretion of the Education Department, and this can be described only as arbitrary. The basic requirements were parental support for the cost of training and maintenance upon commissioning, good social standing, the ability to pass an entrance exam and high-school attendance (although a high-school certificate wasn't required). A conservative upbringing in a middle- or upper-class home was preferred over a formal education. The result was a largely homogeneous officer corps. Most were from northern Germany and, not unsurprisingly, most were from coastal areas. Only some 10–15 per cent were from the nobility, and only 14 per cent were Catholic. Jews were the rare exception, and the sons of social democrats and trade unionists families were excluded.

Upon selection, the candidate was sent to the Navy School for 12 months, followed by exams for executive officer. Next, the candidate undertook another six weeks of specialized training. Now he went to sea for 12 months. If successful, he was commissioned as an ensign. In the final step, the candidate had to be elected to the officer corps by secret ballot by the members of his wardroom. This process offered a last chance to weed out any undesirables. The system was remarkably successful in keeping the officer corps homogeneous. Even under the strains of war, not a single non-commissioned officer was promoted to officer.

In the years before the Great War, and continuing into the war, German naval leadership was never able to solve the growing friction between engineer officers and executive officers. Engineer officers, despite their obvious and growing importance in a modern navy, were treated as second-class citizens, being forced to wear different uniforms and even maintain separate messing from executive officers. By 1917–18, the situation had disintegrated into passive resistance by the engineers.

While the composition of the Royal Navy and German Navy's officer corps was broadly similar, the make-up of the enlisted ranks was vastly different. The Royal Navy relied on volunteers, but the German Navy depended on conscripts to fill the majority of its enlisted ranks. A conscript was obligated for three years' service, followed by another four years in the active reserves. Petty officers were recruited from

German officers and men were as well trained as their Royal Navy counterparts, but operated under a series of restrictive orders from the Kaiser throughout the war. In the end, the Kaiser's prized surface fleet disintegrated into chaos and mutiny.

the most talented seamen. Another difference from the Royal Navy was the creation of a class of rating known as a deck officer. This had no equivalent in the Royal Navy and was required in the German Navy because of the lack of continuity in a conscript force. Despite the title, deck officers were considered ratings, not officers, but to add more confusion they were more like executive officers than senior petty officers in their responsibilities and dress. Advancement to deck officer from petty officer was dependent on technical skill; advancement to commissioned status was extremely remote, and was another source of friction in the personnel ranks. In 1914, there were 2,977 deck officers.

The crew of a German wartime dreadnought was large; for example the crew of *Prinzregent Luitpold* included 22 executive officers, six engineers, two paymasters, 27 deck officers and 1,020 petty officers and ratings. A dreadnought was commanded by an officer of captain rank. The actual running of the ship was performed by the first

ADMIRAL SIR JOHN JELLICOE

If there was ever a man destined for high command in the Royal Navy, it was Admiral Sir John Rushworth Jellicoe. Born in 1859, he entered Britannia Royal Naval College in 1872 at the age of 12. He graduated first in his class, and excelled in all his assignments until being recognized and groomed by Fisher. From that point, he was given important jobs in the Admiralty, which not only prepared him for higher command, but also shaped his view of how he would use that command when he received it. His pre-war billets included Director of Naval Ordnance, Third Sea Lord and Controller (responsible for all ship construction and repairs), commander of the Atlantic Fleet based at Gibraltar, deputy commander of the Home Fleet (later to become the Grand Fleet) and Second Sea Lord (responsible for all personnel matters).

When war seemed unavoidable, Churchill schemed to have Jellicoe take immediate command of the Grand Fleet from Admiral Sir George Callaghan before the scheduled December 1914 handover. Nobody disputed that Jellicoe was the best man for the job, given the range of his experience and his cool powers of analysis combined with a genuine concern for the officers and men under him. Upon assuming command in August 1914 at the age of 55, he became, in the words of Churchill, 'the only man on either side who could lose the war in an afternoon.' Nobody was more aware than Jellicoe of the importance of his role. In the years since 1900, he had come to know several rising officers in the German Navy and he respected the technical prowess of the Germans, especially their gunnery skills. As Director of Naval Ordnance, he realized that German shells, mines and torpedoes were superior to his own. Above all, he was aware of the supreme importance of the Grand Fleet and was determined not to risk it unnecessarily. This view was paramount not only in the run-up to Jutland, during which pressure mounted on him to strike the Germans, but also during the battle itself when he finally had the chance to engage the High Seas Fleet.

VICE ADMIRAL SIR DAVID BEATTY

The other principal British naval figure at Jutland was Vice Admiral Beatty (later admiral), the commander of the Grand Fleet's Battlecruiser Force. As a commander and an officer, he could hardly have been more different than Jellicoe. Beatty was born in 1871 and entered Britannia Royal Naval College in 1884. He graduated in the middle of his class and was in the midst of a mediocre career until the war in Sudan. In 1898, he distinguished himself at the climactic battle of Omdurman, and as a result was promoted early to the rank of commander. In 1899, he was given command of a battleship and was later wounded in China. His experience propelled him to be promoted to captain at the unheard-of age of 29 (the typical age being 42). The next year, he married an American divorcee who was the heiress to the Marshall Fields department store fortune. To say the least, the marriage was challenging for Beatty, who now had to balance his career ambitions with the desires of his demanding wife.

Fisher had also identified Beatty as a future leader of promise, and in 1910 he intervened to have Beatty promoted to admiral at the age of 38. He was now the youngest admiral since Nelson. In 1911, no doubt influenced by his wife, he turned down an appointment as the deputy commander of the Atlantic Fleet. At this point his career looked to be essentially over, until Churchill ended his period of unemployment by taking him as his naval aide. In 1913, he was appointed as the commander of the 1st Battle Cruiser Squadron, the perfect billet for the aggressive Beatty. While he was obviously brave and talented, he was in equal measure rash and impatient. He lacked the technical and professional depth of Jellicoe. When his battlecruisers took a beating from the Germans during the early stages of Jutland, he seemed genuinely surprised that such a vulnerability existed.

VICE ADMIRAL REINHARD SCHEER

On 18 January 1916, Vice Admiral Reinhard Scheer assumed command of the High Seas Fleet. Scheer was an aggressive and confident 53-year-old officer who was determined to take a different course than that of his predecessor.

Scheer joined the navy at 15 from a middle-class background. His early career featured two African tours followed by four years ashore in technical schools, where he specialized in torpedoes. In 1900, he returned to sea as the commander of a destroyer flotilla. Following promotion to captain, he was given command of a battleship in 1907. In 1909, Scheer was appointed to the position of Chief of Staff for the High Seas Fleet, followed the next year by promotion to rear admiral. After a tour as the Chief of the Naval Department, he assumed command of II Squadron, composed of pre-dreadnoughts. In December 1914, he took command of III Squadron consisting of the High Seas Fleet's most powerful dreadnoughts.

Scheer was respected by his peers and subordinates for having a cool and clear mind in action. He was also known for his optimistic outlook. Perhaps this outlook contributed to his determination to seek action with the High Seas Fleet. While an advocate of unrestricted submarine warfare, he did not think that this would be sufficient to defeat Britain. Here was where the High Seas Fleet came into play. It had to put pressure on the British blockade by offensive action. He was not optimistic

Reinhard Scheer, shown second to right with Prince Henry (using binoculars), had the reputation as an aggressive and skilled commander. By any measure, his performance at Jutland was sub-par and he was lucky to bring his fleet back to Germany without much heavier losses.

enough to believe that the High Seas Fleet could defeat the Grand Fleet in an all-out battle, but he was confident that when the time was right to commit the High Seas Fleet to action that its superior ships would allow it to more than hold its own. With this in mind, Scheer presented a more aggressive operational plan to the Kaiser in Wilhelmshaven on 23 February 1916. With the Kaiser's consent, the course was set that would lead to the clash of dreadnoughts at Jutland.

VICE ADMIRAL FRANZ HIPPER

Born in Bavaria in 1863, Hipper joined the navy at age 18 against his mother's wishes. He served briefly overseas, but returned to home waters in 1890 to fulfil his desire to be assigned to the battle fleet. From this point on he served in various units of the High Seas Fleet's scouting forces. He specialized in torpedoes, and commanded a torpedo boat division. In October 1913, he received command of the High Seas Fleet's Scouting Force composed of battlecruisers, light cruisers and destroyers. He served in this role for most of the war up until August 1918, when he succeeded Scheer as commander of the High Seas Fleet.

Hipper was regarded as a tough sea dog, never having served in the Navy Office (the German Admiralty) or attended Staff College. He hated paperwork and was described as being cheerful and light-hearted. His performance during the war was generally excellent. He commanded two raids on the British coast in 1914, before being caught by Beatty in January 1915 at Dogger Bank. Of the four principal admirals at Jutland, only Hipper left the battle with his reputation enhanced – his finely trained and fought battlecruiser force had inflicted most of the damage suffered by the Royal Navy.

officer, who was responsible for all discipline, maintenance and training. Third in command was the navigation officer. Another key figure was the artillery officer, who was responsible for training all gun crews, maintaining all guns and directing the ship's fire in action.

By the time of Jutland, it can be said that massive boredom had begun to affect the High Seas Fleet, but that none of the disciplinary problems which were later to cripple the fleet were yet evident. During the tenure of Admiral von Pohl, which included almost all of 1915, the fleet had gone to sea only five times, and never more than 120 miles from home base. Many of the more adventuresome and ambitious sailors and officers had applied for transfers to the U-boat branch, the air branch or even the army, where they were assured of action. Nevertheless, by all accounts overall morale at Jutland was still high. After Jutland, this would change drastically. By 1917, morale was deplorable; in 1918, the crews of the dreadnoughts went into open mutiny.

Before the war, German dreadnought crews were extremely well drilled and trained, but this fine edge had been tempered by the 22 months leading up to Jutland. Throughout 1915, the German dreadnoughts maintained a dulling schedule: a week on patrol behind the defensive minefields of the Heligoland Bight; another week anchored in the Schilling Roads near Wilhelmshaven, on alert to respond to a British incursion; then a period of gunnery drills in the Kiel Bay, followed by a period of at least two weeks pierside at Wilhelmshaven, where the crews lived ashore. Yet despite the fact that the crews spent less time at sea than British dreadnought crews, in May 1916 the gunnery skills of the Germans remained high, with gun crews able to get the range quickly and maintain a high rate of fire.

COMBAT

BRITISH AND GERMAN TACTICS

It is important to review the general tactics of each side before beginning an account of the battle itself. The tactics of the Grand Fleet were developed entirely by Jellicoe and were built on three precepts. The first, and most important, was a defensive emphasis. Jellicoe was determined not to risk his dreadnoughts to underwater threats. He was convinced that the Germans would operate their submarines in conjunction with their battle fleet and that a German tactic would be to lay mines and then attempt to draw the British across them. Jellicoe also gave the Germans credit for a formidable destroyer force equipped with superior torpedoes. Thus, he intended to engage the Germans with gunfire at long ranges, beyond the effective range of torpedoes.

To keep his fleet together and to bring the greatest number of heavy guns to bear on the enemy, Jellicoe was also determined to fight in a line-ahead formation on a

A G-37-class German destroyer cutting through a line of High Seas Fleet dreadnoughts. The British overestimated the torpedo threat posed by German light units during the war and this perception affected their tactics at Jutland. During the battle, German torpedo boats played only a minor role.

parallel course to the enemy. He rejected more flexible tactics due to his concern that a squadron of the Grand Fleet might be isolated and destroyed, and his doubt that 'divided' tactics could be employed successfully. Because the threat of torpedoes made it too dangerous to steam in a line ahead during the approach phase, Jellicoe ordered that the Grand Fleet approach the enemy in columns. He would order the fleet to deploy into a line ahead just before the battle was joined. He desired that the engagement begin at long range (18,000 yards) and that in the early stages he would not close inside 14,000 yards. Once the weight of gunfire had reduced German strength, he would close to 10,000 yards to finish the enemy. British destroyers were to be employed in an entirely defensive role. Jellicoe's third precept was simple – the Grand Fleet would rely on centralized control: him.

ORDER OF BATTLE – JUTLAND 1916

THE GRAND FLEET

Battle fleet

1st Battle Squadron
  5th Division: *Colossus, Collingwood, Neptune, St Vincent*
  6th Division: *Marlborough, Revenge, Hercules, Agincourt*
2nd Battle Squadron
  1st Division: *King George V, Ajax, Centurion, Erin*
  2nd Division: *Orion, Monarch, Conqueror, Thunderer*
4th Battle Squadron
  3rd Division: *Iron Duke, Royal Oak, Superb, Canada*
  4th Division: *Benbow, Bellerophon, Temeraire, Vanguard*
3rd Battle Cruiser Squadron (temporarily attached)
  Invincible, Inflexible, Indomitable
Armoured cruisers: 8
Light cruisers: 12
Destroyers: 51
Minelayer: 1

Battle Cruiser Fleet

Battlecruiser *Lion*
1st Battle Cruiser Squadron
  Princess Royal, Queen Mary, Tiger
2nd Battle Cruiser Squadron
  New Zealand, Indefatigable

5th Battle Cruiser Squadron (temporarily attached)
  Barham, Valiant, Warspite, Malaya
Light cruisers: 14
Destroyers: 28
Seaplane carrier: 1

HIGH SEAS FLEET

Battle fleet

I Battle Squadron
  I Division: *Ostfriesland, Thüringen, Helgoland, Oldenburg*
  II Division: *Posen, Rheinland, Nassau, Westfalen*
II Battle Squadron (6 pre-dreadnoughts)
III Battle Squadron
  V Division: *König, Grosser Kurfürst, Kronprinz, Markgraf*
  VI Division: *Kaiser, Kaiserin, Prinzregent Luitpold Friedrich der Grosse*
Light cruisers: 6
Torpedo boats: 32

Scouting Force

I Scouting Group
  Battlecruisers *Lutzow, Derfflinger, Seydlitz, Moltke, Von der Tann*
Light cruisers: 5
Torpedo boats: 30

Despite Jellicoe's concerns, German tactics were also dedicated to a decisive gunnery engagement. Yet Scheer, being a torpedo expert, did see a role for a massed destroyer attack under some circumstances. Scheer planned to isolate and destroy a small portion of the Grand Fleet; under no circumstances did he want to be drawn into a decisive engagement with the main body of the enemy fleet. Should this appear to be happening, Scheer planned to resort to an evasive turn away covered by smoke and a torpedo attack.

Scheer's tactics in the battle itself were driven by the fact that he was heavily outnumbered; in dreadnoughts the edge was 28 to 16 and 9 to 5 in battlecruisers, favouring the British. This translated into a significant British advantage in

Opening movements of the battle of Jutland, 31 May 1916

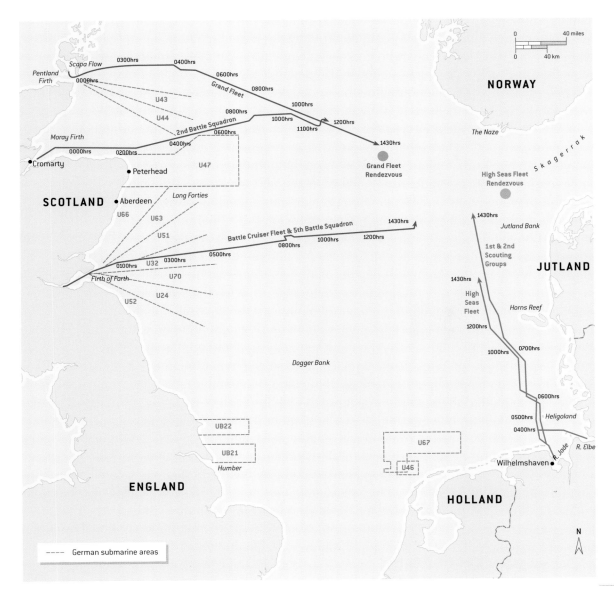

firepower as well. The British dreadnoughts carried a total of 272 heavy guns, while the German dreadnoughts brought 200 heavy guns to the fight. Battlecruiser firepower was also stacked in favour of the British, with 72 heavy guns against 44 for the Germans. To top off Scheer's challenge, the British had a general speed advantage. Because Scheer had relented and decided to bring the pre-dreadnoughts of II Battle Squadron with the High Seas Fleet, he was restricted to a maximum speed of 18 knots, which was 2–3 knots slower than the Grand Fleet. Likewise, the newest of Beatty's battlecruisers possessed a 3-knot advantage over Hipper's formation.

FIRST CONTACT

By 28 May 1916, Room 40 had provided ample evidence that something unusual was stirring in the North Sea. On 30 May, it appeared that a major operation by the High Seas Fleet was imminent. In reaction, the Admiralty brought the Grand Fleet to readiness that afternoon. That evening, Jellicoe led the bulk of the Grand Fleet (16 dreadnoughts and three battlecruisers) out from Scapa Flow, soon to be joined by another eight dreadnoughts from Cromarty. Beatty's Battle Cruiser Fleet departed the Firth of Forth with six battlecruisers and the four fast dreadnoughts of the 5th Battle Squadron.

Since the High Seas Fleet did not leave until early on the morning of 31 May, the British had beaten the Germans to sea, but their departure was far from incident free. As the Grand Fleet steamed at an economical 15 knots, zigzagging due to the threat of submarines, Jellicoe received a signal from the Admiralty at 1248hrs incorrectly informing him that the Germans were not at sea. This gross error was the result of poor judgement from the Director of the Operations Division at the Admiralty. It was also a crucial error; had Jellicoe been informed that the Germans were at sea, he could have increased his speed to engage the Germans earlier in the day. Perhaps more importantly, when Jellicoe received subsequent information from the Admiralty on the Germans' location, he tended to ignore it.

The greatest clash of dreadnoughts in history began innocently enough. The light cruiser *Galatea* on Beatty's port wing spotted a plume of smoke 8 miles away – this was a Danish freighter blowing off steam. Upon investigating the contact, *Galatea* reported two German warships, which were also investigating the smoke, and sent a report to Beatty at 1420hrs. Beatty reacted quickly and ordered his fleet to go to battle stations, increase speed to 22 knots and head to the south-east to cut the Germans off from their bases. A communications failure, however, separated the four dreadnoughts of the 5th Battle Squadron from Beatty's battlecruisers.

As the respective battlecruiser fleets joined for battle, the opposing dreadnought forces were hours away. Jellicoe was some 65 miles to the north, at least three hours' steaming time. In response to *Galatea's* messages that the German force included battlecruisers, he increased speed to 19 knots. Scheer was some 50 miles to the south.

THE BATTLECRUISER PHASE

Hipper spotted the British battlecruisers first. He reversed his course to the south to draw the unwary British upon Scheer's dreadnoughts. Beatty was more than willing to give chase. By his observations, his force faced only five German battlecruisers. With a 10–5 advantage in capital ships and superior speed, he was sure that a decisive victory was at hand. For the next hour, from 1545 until 1640hrs, the battlecruisers would slug it out supported by the four super-dreadnoughts of the 5th Battle Squadron.

When the range reached 16,500 yards, Beatty swung his six battlecruisers into line to engage the Germans. The 5th Battle Squadron was now some 7 miles behind. Hipper's battlecruisers were on a parallel course to the south-east, and they opened fire at about the same time. From the start, German gunnery was excellent. The first salvo was 200 yards short, but the next straddled its targets, gaining early hits. Within minutes, three of the British battlecruisers had been hit multiple times. The British, facing unfavourable light conditions, and handicapped by smoke, overshot consistently. By 1555hrs, the range was down to 13,000 yards.

The excellent German shooting was soon rewarded. At 1603hrs, after being struck by two salvoes from the battlecruiser *Von der Tann*, *Indefatigable* blew up, killing 1,017 of her crew. Beatty's flagship *Lion* was hit multiple times and avoided the fate of *Indefatigable* by flooding the magazine of her amidships 13.5in turret. The accurate German fire forced Beatty to open the range to 18,000 yards.

Making 24.5 knots, the four ships of the 5th Battle Squadron struggled to get into range. Finally, at 1610hrs, they brought their 15in guns to bear and gained quick hits on two German battlecruisers. Yet this fire did not stop battlecruisers *Derfflinger* and *Seydlitz* from concentrating a bombardment on the battlecruiser *Queen Mary*. Hit in her amidships magazine, she blew up at 1626hrs with the loss of all but eight of her crew of 1,274. Her destruction was witnessed by the navigating officer on the battlecruiser *New Zealand*:

Seydlitz was typical of the German approach to battlecruiser design, with an emphasis on protection. Her 11in main belt armour made her as well protected as most British battleships. Accordingly, the Germans never felt the need to design a squadron of fast battleships like the Royal Navy's *Queen Elizabeth* class.

Malaya was assigned to the 5th Battle Squadron and was in the thick of the fighting at Jutland. She fired 215 rounds at the Germans, with good results. In return, she received eight hits by heavy shells, but suffered no major damage. However, 63 of her crew were killed and another 68 wounded.

… suddenly I saw a salvo hit *Queen Mary* on her port side. A small cloud of what looked like coal-dust came out from where she was hit, but nothing more until several moments later, when a terrific yellow flame with a heavy and very dense mass of black smoke showed ahead, and the *Queen Mary* herself was no longer visible.

In an effort to bring relief to his heavy ships, Beatty ordered 12 destroyers to deliver torpedo attacks on the German battlecruisers. These attacks were countered by Hipper, who ordered a light cruiser and 15 destroyers to attack the British heavy ships.

OPPOSITE: Fleet Action 1830–1835hrs

GERMAN GUNSIGHT VIEW

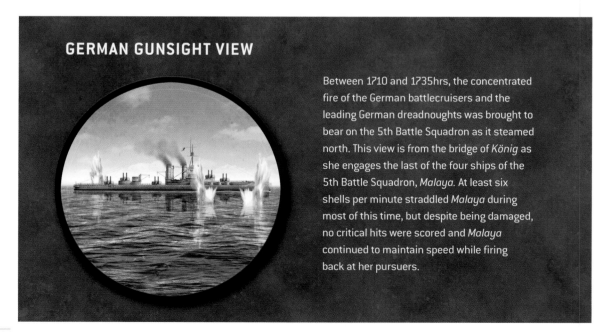

Between 1710 and 1735hrs, the concentrated fire of the German battlecruisers and the leading German dreadnoughts was brought to bear on the 5th Battle Squadron as it steamed north. This view is from the bridge of *König* as she engages the last of the four ships of the 5th Battle Squadron, *Malaya*. At least six shells per minute straddled *Malaya* during most of this time, but despite being damaged, no critical hits were scored and *Malaya* continued to maintain speed while firing back at her pursuers.

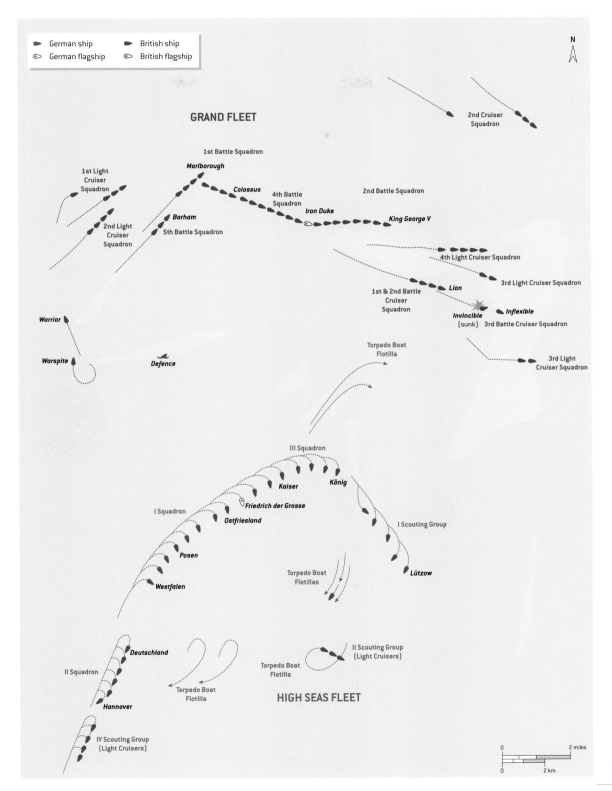

German ship · British ship
German flagship · British flagship

N

GRAND FLEET

2nd Cruiser Squadron

1st Battle Squadron
Marlborough

1st Light Cruiser Squadron

Colossus

4th Battle Squadron

2nd Battle Squadron

Barham

Iron Duke

King George V

2nd Light Cruiser Squadron

5th Battle Squadron

4th Light Cruiser Squadron

3rd Light Cruiser Squadron

1st & 2nd Battle Cruiser Squadron

Lion

Warrior

Invincible (sunk)

Inflexible

3rd Battle Cruiser Squadron

Warspite

Defence

Torpedo Boat Flotilla

3rd Light Cruiser Squadron

III Squadron

Kaiser

König

I Squadron

Friedrich der Grosse

Ostfriesland

I Scouting Group

Posen

Torpedo Boat Flotillas

Westfalen

Lützow

Deutschland

II Scouting Group (Light Cruisers)

II Squadron

Torpedo Boat Flotilla

Hannover

Torpedo Boat Flotilla

HIGH SEAS FLEET

IV Scouting Group (Light Cruisers)

0 — 2 miles
0 — 2 km

In the ensuing mêlée, two destroyers on each side were sunk and one British torpedo found its mark on *Seydlitz*, but her effective anti-torpedo defences allowed her to maintain speed and stay in line.

As bad as Beatty's problems appeared to be, they got worse at 1638hrs when he received a signal from one of his light cruiser squadrons that it had sighted the High Seas Fleet. Now Beatty faced the strength of both Hipper and Scheer, and Jellicoe's battleships were still 50 miles away. He changed course to the north at 1640hrs to draw the Germans into the Grand Fleet. At this point, more signalling problems bedevilled the British. The 5th Battle Squadron missed the original order to turn north, and it was not repeated and acknowledged for another 14 minutes. All this time, the 5th Battle Squadron continued towards the 16 dreadnoughts of the High Seas Fleet. A turret officer onboard *Malaya* recalled the spectacle:

> I saw, just distinguishable in the mist, a warship of sorts coming from the S.E... We were not long kept in suspense as to what this new ship was, for very shortly after sighting her, I saw following her a long line of others, which we soon recognized as German Dreadnought Battleships of the König and Kaiser classes.

When the turn was made in full view of the German battleline, both *Barham* and *Warspite* were hit. Beatty's battlecruisers were severely battered, but none had any damage to their engineering plants so were able to use their superior speed to pull away. Left behind, the four ships of the 5th Battle Squadron faced the concentrated fire of Hipper's five battlecruisers and the lead ships of the High Seas Fleet, the four König class dreadnoughts. Both *Malaya* and *Barham* were hit another five times. This was the time of maximum peril for the finest of the Royal Navy's dreadnoughts, as this account from *Warspite*'s executive officer affirms:

> Very soon after the turn I suddenly saw on the starboard quarter the whole of the High Seas Fleet; at least I saw masts, funnels, and an endless ripple of orange flashes all down the line, how many I didn't try to count, as we were getting well strafed at this time, but I remember counting up to eight. The noise of their shells over and short was deafening...

Scheer still had no idea that the Grand Fleet was at sea and was just over the horizon. In response to what appeared to be a British flight and eager to consolidate

his apparent victory, he ordered 'Give Chase' at 1720hrs. This pursuit had the effect of stringing out the High Seas Fleet. The 'Run to the North' ended at 1745hrs, when Beatty spotted the advance units of the Grand Fleet. Beatty now changed course to the east to disguise the arrival of Jellicoe's force for as long as possible. At 1755hrs, however, a German light cruiser reported British battleships to the east. Minutes later, the leading German dreadnoughts sighted 24 British dreadnoughts spread out across the northern horizon. Scheer's worst nightmare had been realized – the entire strength of the Grand Fleet was only 16,000 yards away and closing.

THE BATTLELINES ENGAGE

After Jellicoe dispatched Rear Admiral Sir Horace Hood's 3rd Battle Cruiser Squadron to support Beatty at 1605hrs, he went into an information void. He knew that Beatty was engaging the High Seas Fleet and that the action was moving north to his position, but Beatty had utterly failed to keep him informed of the details of the battlecruiser action and did not inform Jellicoe of the location and movement of the German fleet. From 1645hrs until just after 1800hrs, Beatty sent Jellicoe no communications. Jellicoe was forced to rely on what little he could see from his flagship *Iron Duke*. An intermittent haze persisted throughout the day, which created variable visibility sometimes up to 16,000 yards, other times down to a mere 2,000 yards.

By 1800hrs, Jellicoe could finally see Beatty's flagship, but it was obvious that the pursuing Germans were closer than he anticipated. Now he had a difficult decision to make on how to deploy his force. The Grand Fleet was steaming south in six columns, each with four dreadnoughts. Jellicoe needed to direct his fleet into a line-ahead formation to bring his big guns to bear on the Germans. Deployment into a line ahead would take 20 minutes, and once begun it could not be stopped. If Jellicoe deployed his ships to starboard (to the west), he would place his dreadnoughts closer to where he thought the Germans were, thus allowing him to open fire sooner. On the other hand, such a deployment also ran the risk of bringing his fleet immediately into

OVERLEAF
By 1830hrs, the main fleet action was under way. The 6th Division of the 1st Battle Squadron was heavily engaged. Shown here are the four ships of the division with their guns trained to starboard. The leading ship is *Marlborough* (Iron Duke class with 13.5in guns) followed by *Revenge* (with 15in guns), then *Hercules* (12in guns) and finally *Agincourt* (the only British dreadnought with 14in guns).

German torpedo range. If Jellicoe deployed to port (to the east), he would end up some 4,000 yards farther away from the Germans. This manoeuvre would also have the effect of crossing Scheer's 'T', and place the British in a favourable light situation where they would be hidden in the mists to the east and the Germans silhouetted against the sunset in the west. Historians have debated this choice ever since, but Jellicoe had only minutes to decide. He chose to go to port.

While Jellicoe's 24 dreadnoughts began to deploy into their fighting formation, Beatty's force steamed across Jellicoe's to take up its position at the front of the formation. The commander of the 5th Battle Squadron decided to move his ships to the rear of the British line. During this manoeuvre, *Warspite* suffered a jammed rudder that forced her to make two complete circles within 8,000 yards of the German dreadnoughts. The Germans concentrated a furious fire on the British ship; due to her heavy armour, however, and good fortune, none of the 13 hits inflicted serious damage. Unable to manoeuvre, *Warspite* was out of the fight and was ordered to return to Rosyth.

In the van of the Grand Fleet's formation were two squadrons of armoured cruisers. Now, half of the 1st Battle Cruiser Squadron found itself within 8,000 yards of the German dreadnoughts. The Germans made quick work of the armoured cruiser *Defence*, which blew up and sank at 1820hrs together with her crew of 900; a second armored cruiser, *Warrior*, was also taken under fire and mortally damaged. She sank the following morning. An observer aboard *Colossus* described the demise of *Defence*:

> At about 6.15p.m. we witnessed the action of the 1st Cruiser Squadron and the blowing up of *Defence*. We thought she had gone about a minute before she finally blew up, as she completely disappeared in a mass of spray, smoke, and flame. But she came through it apparently still intact, only to disappear later in a tremendous belch of vivid flame and dense black smoke, from which some dark object, possibly a boat or a funnel, was hurled through space, twirling like a gigantic Catherine-wheel.

As the German battleships were pummelling the armoured cruisers, the 3rd Battle Cruiser Squadron joined the fray. The three battlecruisers were on a parallel course

Oldenburg pictured during the battle of Jutland firing her main armament. She fired only 53 main battery rounds during the battle and was hit by a single secondary round, which killed eight and wounded 14.

with Hipper's battlecruisers at about 9,000 yards. Having just returned from gunnery practice at Scapa Flow, the British battlecruisers opened an impressive fire on the leading two German battlecruisers. After scoring heavily against *Lutzow*, *Invincible* was engaged by *Derfflinger*. On the third salvo, the British battlecruiser was struck amidships and for a third time the horrible scene of a British battlecruiser blowing up was repeated. The 12in German shell ignited the powder in the hoist, which travelled down the trunk to the magazines. *Invincible* exploded; only six men were rescued of a crew of 1,032.

Screened by the 3rd Battle Cruiser Squadron, the Grand Fleet was deploying into its line-ahead formation, crossing the 'T' of the German dreadnoughts. This positioning would allow the British dreadnoughts to use their entire broadside, while allowing the Germans to employ only those heavy guns that could be brought to bear forwards. Here was the moment the Royal Navy had been planning for since the war began. Yet it did not turn out to be the crushing blow for which the British had hoped. Coming into the line ahead, no organized fire distribution was possible. The first dreadnought, *Marlborough*, opened fire at 1817hrs, but most ships did not even open fire until 1830hrs. Even then, only ten, maybe 12, of the 24 dreadnoughts fired on the Germans. Visibility was poor and correction of fire difficult. The target for this onslaught was Hipper's battlecruisers and the dreadnoughts of III Squadron. *König* was especially hard hit by eight heavy shells.

As the volume of British fire increased, the Germans were unable to find targets in the poor light to hit back effectively. Scheer was now in a critical situation. Jellicoe had crossed his 'T' and the British dreadnoughts were delivering a withering fire. He was 150 miles from home with the British fleet between him and safety, and his fleet was inferior in speed to the British. To stay and slug it out with the Grand Fleet would only invite disaster. The captain of battlecruiser *Seydlitz* described the situation:

Visibility had gradually become very unfavourable. There was a dense mist, so that as a rule only the flashes of the enemy's guns, but not the ships themselves, could be seen. From northwest to northeast we had before us a hostile line firing its guns, though in the mist we could only glimpse the flashes from time to time. It was a mighty and terrible spectacle.

At 1833hrs, Scheer ordered a manoeuvre practised for just such an occasion. Called the 'battle about-turn', it required each ship to make a simultaneous 180-degree turn. On this occasion, the High Seas Fleet executed the manoeuvre smartly; all 22 dreadnoughts and pre-dreadnoughts turned away from the Grand Fleet and disappeared, aided by a smokescreen laid by German destroyers and favourable winds.

Scheer's turn had been executed even before the Grand Fleet could deploy all its dreadnoughts into a line ahead. Thus, the long-awaited main action had lasted only some 20 minutes from 1815 until 1835hrs. Jellicoe decided not to follow the Germans into the mist, and by 1855hrs was still unsure what had happened. At 1857hrs a torpedo struck *Marlborough*, an incident that probably served to reinforce Jellicoe's reluctance to chase the Germans. He maintained course to the south-east and then to the south to keep the Grand Fleet between the Germans and their bases. Eventually, the Germans would have to come to him.

THE SECOND ENGAGEMENT

At 1855hrs Scheer inexplicably ordered a second battle about-turn at 1855hrs. Though he had broken contact with the British, he ordered the High Seas Fleet right back into the massed fire of the Grand Fleet. The reasons for this order have never been adequately explained, even by Scheer himself. Perhaps he hoped to surprise the

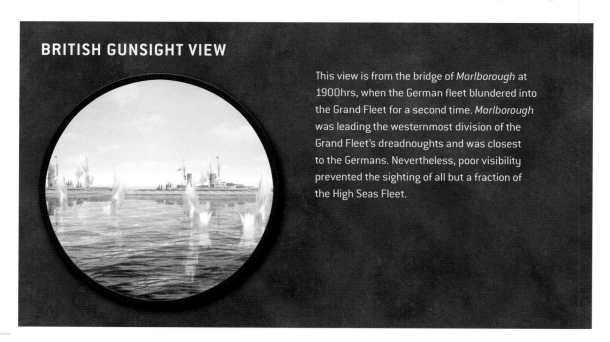

BRITISH GUNSIGHT VIEW

This view is from the bridge of *Marlborough* at 1900hrs, when the German fleet blundered into the Grand Fleet for a second time. *Marlborough* was leading the westernmost division of the Grand Fleet's dreadnoughts and was closest to the Germans. Nevertheless, poor visibility prevented the sighting of all but a fraction of the High Seas Fleet.

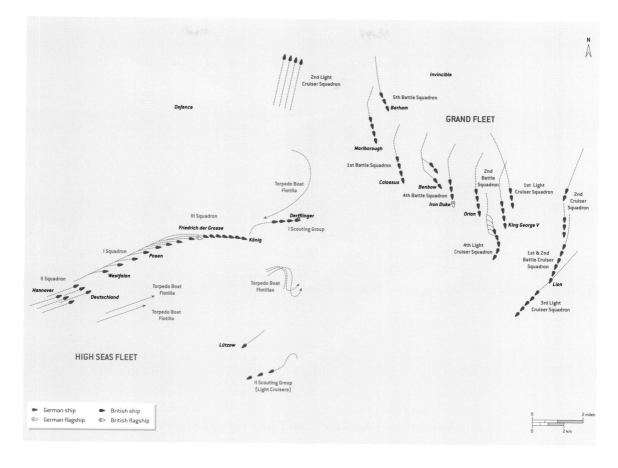

Labels on map:

2nd Light Cruiser Squadron
Invincible
Defence
5th Battle Squadron
Barham
GRAND FLEET
Marlborough
1st Battle Squadron
Torpedo Boat Flotilla
Colossus
Benbow
2nd Battle Squadron
1st Light Cruiser Squadron
2nd Cruiser Squadron
4th Battle Squadron
Iron Duke
III Squadron
Derfflinger
Friedrich der Grosse
I Scouting Group
Orion
Konig
King George V
I Squadron
Posen
4th Light Cruiser Squadron
1st & 2nd Battle Cruiser Squadron
II Squadron
Westfalen
Torpedo Boat Flotilla
Torpedo Boat Flotillas
Lion
Hannover
Deutschland
Torpedo Boat Flotilla
Torpedo Boat Flotillas
3rd Light Cruiser Squadron
Lützow
HIGH SEAS FLEET
II Scouting Group (Light Cruisers)

German ship   British ship
German flagship   British flagship

0   2 miles
0   2 km

British or break through to the east and head for home. None of this happened. When the German fleet reappeared out of the mist, the British quickly responded.

By 1915hrs, the entire Grand Fleet was pouring fire on the High Seas Fleet from a range of between 11,000 and 14,000 yards. Again the van of Scheer's fleet was hammered and was unable to respond effectively. The only damage suffered by the British was two hits on the battleship *Colossus* that caused minor damage and wounded five men. Of note, these were the only gunfire casualties suffered by any Grand Fleet dreadnought during the entire battle. In contrast, during this phase in the clash the British hit the Germans with 37 large-calibre shells.

For a second time, Scheer was faced with an immediate decision to save his fleet. He ordered the fleet to prepare to execute another battle about-turn. This was to be covered by an advance by Hipper's battlecruisers to cover the withdrawal and by a massed destroyer attack. At 1913hrs, Hipper's battered battlecruisers began their charge against the Grand Fleet. Though it lasted for only four minutes, this 'death ride' constituted one of the most dramatic and controversial moments of the battle. The death ride was followed by an attack by 14 destroyers, aimed at the Grand Fleet's dreadnoughts. The destroyers came to within 8,000 yards of the British battleline before launching 31 torpedoes. An observer aboard *Conqueror* described the action:

Fleet Action 1910–1915hrs

At 7.14 observed enemy destroyers attacking, and fired on them for eight minutes. They were making a very heavy smoke screen, and were never on the same course for more than a minute at a time, turning, twisting, wriggling, and disappearing into their own smoke, only to reappear again almost immediately at a different place.

Now Jellicoe was forced to make an instant decision that would have great impact on the course of the battle. In order to present a much smaller target to the approaching torpedoes, he could either turn his dreadnoughts into them or turn away from them. If he turned into them, the speed of the advancing torpedoes combined with the speed of his own ships would leave little margin for error in executing evasive manoeuvres. It would, however, place him in an excellent position to resume the pursuit of the now disorganized German fleet. If he turned away, the closing speed of the torpedoes would be much reduced and many would probably run out of fuel before reaching their intended targets. While preserving the Grand Fleet's dreadnoughts from underwater damage, the eventuality most feared by Jellicoe, it would allow the German fleet to get away.

In the most single controversial decision of the battle, Jellicoe chose to turn away from the Germans. The manoeuvre was successful in defeating the German torpedo attack – only 21 torpedoes reached the British dreadnoughts, and, despite several close calls, none hit their target. The tactical cost, however, was high; Scheer's desperate counterattacks allowed him to disengage just as it appeared that the High Seas Fleet was about to be smashed by the Grand Fleet's overwhelming gun power. Again, following this turn away, Jellicoe did not know where Scheer was. In fact, he had broken contact and was 15 miles away. Yet as night fell, the British were still between the High Seas Fleet and home. Jellicoe had every expectation that the next morning would see the destruction of the German fleet.

THE HIGH SEAS FLEET BREAKS THROUGH

Given what he perceived as German advantages in both training and equipment for night combat, Jellicoe had no desire to seek an engagement with the Germans until daylight. After 2100hrs, he returned the Grand Fleet to cruising formation. Since he still believed the German fleet to be located to his north-west, Jellicoe deployed all of his destroyers behind his dreadnoughts to deal with any German night torpedo attack against his vulnerable heavy ships.

Jellicoe had reason to be concerned about a night action. In addition to the German superiority in torpedoes, the Germans had trained heavily for night engagements. They possessed larger and better searchlights and had incorporated them into their night gunnery techniques. Though confident of the night-fighting capabilities of his ships, however, Scheer had only one thought in mind – escape. He would have to act quickly, as dawn would break at 0200hrs and full daylight would be reached an hour later.

There were several potential routes for Scheer to take through the German and British minefields to get home. One was the long route around Denmark to the Baltic. This option was immediately dismissed as too long, especially given that many German ships were damaged. The closest route to the current location of the German fleet was south-east to the Horns Reef lightship and then south behind the minefields of the Amrum Bank. This was the route Scheer had taken en route to battle on 31 May. The other possibilities called for the Germans to steer south-west towards the Ems River and then head east to Wilhelmshaven, or to steer south towards Heligoland and then home. For his part, Jellicoe doubted that the Germans would attempt to break through the British fleet again to reach Horns Reef, so he decided to head south. Scheer knew that the Grand Fleet was located to his south-east, so an escape to the south seemed out of the question. He decided to take the shortest way home via Horns Reef, now only 85 miles away, by passing astern of the Grand Fleet. At 2110hrs he gave orders to steer to the south-east at 16 knots, stopping at nothing until Horns Reef was reached. He asked for airship reconnaissance of the Horns Reef area at daybreak. The undamaged dreadnoughts *Westfalen, Nassau, Rheinland* and *Posen* moved into the van to lead the breakthrough.

What transpired on the night on 31 May to 1 June was a series of confusing and savage clashes between the British destroyer flotillas and the heavy units of the High Seas Fleet. The German destroyers, feared by Jellicoe, played no role in the combat. The most remarkable aspect of the night battle was the universal lack of initiative shown by the dreadnoughts of the Grand Fleet and the critical lack of professionalism exhibited by the Admiralty in passing intelligence to Jellicoe, intelligence that could have changed the battle.

As the two fleets converged, with the Grand Fleet heading south at 17 knots and the High Seas Fleet heading south-east at 16 knots, the first elements to make contact were the fleet's respective scouting forces of light cruisers. In a clash at less than 1,000 yards, an old German light cruiser was sunk and a British light cruiser was heavily damaged. Jellicoe still had no reason to believe that the Germans were not heading south. He interpreted the sound of combat to his rear as the expected clash between destroyers. Even at 2241hrs, a message from the Admiralty that contained the contents of Scheer's 2110hrs orders failed to change his plans. By this time, after a series of misleading or simply incorrect reports, Jellicoe's confidence in intelligence provided by the Admiralty had reached its nadir. Inexplicably, the Admiralty failed to forward to Jellicoe Scheer's request for airship reconnaissance of Horns Reef. Had this been done, Jellicoe would have been in no doubt about the Germans' intended escape route. Even more inexcusable was the fact that the airship message was only one of seven messages intercepted and deciphered by Room 40 which gave the High Seas Fleet's course or position between 1043 and 0100hrs. None of these were passed by the Admiralty to Jellicoe.

By 2230hrs, Scheer's dreadnoughts began encountering the British destroyers in the rear of the Grand Fleet's formation. In a series of close-range clashes, the 4th Destroyer Flotilla was battered by the leading German battleships. Four British destroyers were sunk or left sinking, and another three were heavily damaged. One of these was rammed by the dreadnought *Nassau*, but was able to return home despite losing 60ft of plating from the side of her hull. In return, the British destroyers torpedoed a German light cruiser, which was later abandoned. Another German light cruiser collided with the dreadnought *Posen* and was later abandoned. The sacrifice of the destroyers was in vain; none made a contact report to Jellicoe. More inexplicable was the fact that the several British dreadnoughts that identified the German battleships moving east neither engaged them nor made a contact report.

Later, the armoured cruiser *Black Prince* came across three dreadnoughts of Scheer's I Squadron, including his flagship *Friedrich der Grosse*. The dreadnoughts engaged the poorly armoured cruiser at point-blank range. *Black Prince* blew up with the loss of her entire crew of 900. At about 0145hrs, the Germans encountered another group of British destroyers from the 12th Flotilla. These were able to fire 17 torpedoes at the German heavy ships at a range of only 2,000–3,000 yards. None of the dreadnoughts were hit, but pre-dreadnought *Pommern* was struck by a single torpedo, causing a catastrophic explosion that destroyed the ship and killed all 844 aboard. This is how the action looked from one of the British destroyers:

> At 2 minutes past 2 the *Faulknor* fired her first torpedo, which probably passed ahead of the second enemy ship… About two minutes later the second torpedo was fired, but almost simultaneously with this the Germans sighted our flotilla, and all their battleships opened fire, together with the light cruisers astern of their line who poured a particularly heavy fire on us. The sea seemed to be alive with bursting shells and the air with the whistle of passing projectiles. The range was if anything under 1,500 yards, and 'overs' much predominated. Suddenly a huge explosion took place on the third German ship, and with a deafening noise and shock she seemed first of all to open out, then to close together, then to go.

With this final action, Scheer had broken through the Grand Fleet. At no time did Jellicoe receive a report of German dreadnoughts being engaged. All present on *Iron Duke*'s bridge continued to believe that the sounds of combat and periodic flash of searchlights to the north was nothing more than a series of destroyer actions. Finally at 0230hrs, Jellicoe moved his fleet towards Horns Reef, but it was too late to catch the Germans outside of their protective minefields.

By 1300hrs on 1 June, leading elements of the High Seas Fleet reached the mouth of the Jade and Elbe. The dreadnought *Ostfriesland* struck a mine at 0520hrs, but continued south and reached home. Even four of Hipper's battlecruisers were able to penetrate the British formation and reach safety. The exception was *Lutzow*, which was finally abandoned and scuttled. *Seydlitz* was spotted and identified by no less than four British dreadnoughts, but none engaged the helpless battlecruiser, which had to be eventually towed stern-first into harbour with thousands of tons of water aboard.

At about 0400hrs, Jellicoe received a message from the Admiralty that contained Scheer's 0230hrs position only 16 miles from Horns Reef lightship. This message confirmed what Jellicoe already suspected – he had lost his opportunity to finish off the Germans. All that was left was to sweep north looking for stragglers (none was found) and then head back to Scapa Flow where the Grand Fleet arrived at noon on 2 June.

STATISTICS AND ANALYSIS

Most analysis of the battle of Jutland starts with the numbers of ships and men lost by each side. Yet strategically, this misses the point. The battle changed nothing with regards to the overall situation at sea. Whatever tactical success the Germans could claim, the blockade of Germany remained intact. The most succinct commentary about the battle was attributed to a journalist who offered, 'The German fleet had assaulted its jailer and

König was the most heavily damaged German dreadnought during the battle. This view shows damage from a British heavy shell, which has penetrated the deck armour in the area of the forward turret.

Losses at Jutland		
	British	German
Battlecruisers	*Queen Mary* *Invincible* *Indefatigable*	*Lutzow*
Pre-dreadnought		*Pommern*
Armoured cruisers	*Defence* *Warrior* *Back Prince*	
Light cruisers		*Wiesbaden* *Frauenlob* *Elbing* *Rostock*
Destroyers	8	5
Killed	6,094	2,551
Wounded	674	507
Prisoner	177	0
Total casualties	6,945	3,058

was back in jail.' This strategic result was not lost on Scheer, who delivered a report to the Kaiser on 4 July 1916. While laudatory on the achievements of the High Seas Fleet, the report made the central assertion that victory was not possible at sea against the Grand Fleet. In his view, given the numerical dreadnought superiority of the British and Germany's unfavourable geographic position, resumption of the U-boat campaign against British shipping was the only way to victory.

Nevertheless, on a tactical level, the outcome of the battle was much different. The Germans had more than held their own, and a simple tally of losses suggested that they could claim victory.

Simply tallying up losses also misses the point. The High Seas Fleet did not gain a victory as much as it had avoided annihilation. While the Grand Fleet reported itself ready for sea on the evening of 2 June with 22 of its 24 dreadnoughts, the High Seas Fleet limped back to Wilhelmshaven. Of the 16 dreadnoughts that participated, only eight were fit for action after the battle. Of the five battlecruisers, only two remained ready for operations some two months later. The vast majority of the damage to the Grand Fleet was suffered by the battlecruiser force and its attached 5th Battle Squadron. Moreover, any losses that the Grand Fleet suffered were made up by the return of the dreadnoughts *Queen Elizabeth* and *Emperor of India* from refit, and the addition of the three last units of the Revenge class.

The extent of damage suffered by the principal units of both sides, damage that required dry-docking to be repaired, can be gauged by the table below.

In addition, several other German dreadnoughts were damaged but did not require dry-docking. These included *Rheinland* (damage completed by 10 June), *Westfalen* (completed 17 June) and *Nassau* (completed 10 July).

Battleship and battlecruisers damaged, with repair completion dates			
German	Completion date	British	Completion date
Helgoland	16 June	*Tiger*	1 July
Grosser Kurfürst	16 July	*Barham*	4 July
Markgraf	20 July	*Malaya*	10 July
König	21 July	*Warspite*	20 July
Ostfriesland	26 July	*Princess Royal*	21 July
Moltke	39 July	*Marlborough*	2 August
Von der Tann	2 August	*Lion*	13 September
Seydlitz	16 September		
Derfflinger	15 October		

The edge in gunnery accuracy, statistically, goes to the Germans. A total of about 85 heavy shells fired by German battleships and battlecruisers struck their British opponents. In contrast, 102 heavy British shells struck German dreadnoughts or battlecruisers.

The most thorough analysis of the battle indicates that gunnery on neither side was outstanding. After hits to smaller ships are factored in, the total accuracy for the British heavy guns was 2.75 per cent (123 hits out of 4,480 rounds fired). For the Germans, the total accuracy was a bit better at 3.39 per cent (122 hits out of 3,597 fired). If the 12 hits on the armoured cruiser *Black Prince* are discounted (these were scored at point-blank range), the overall accuracy drops to 3.08 per cent. For the High Seas Fleet, the most accurate ships were the well-drilled battlecruisers, with an overall accuracy of 3.89 per cent (65 out of 1,670). The German dreadnoughts scored a less impressive 2.96 per cent (57 of 1,927), even with the estimated 12 hits on *Black Prince* included. This disparity was due in large measure to the fact that the battlecruisers were heavily engaged earlier in the battle when light conditions favoured the Germans and overall visibility was better.

For the British, the battlecruisers of the 1st and 2nd Battle Squadrons exhibited an overall dismal accuracy rate of 1.43 per cent of the 1,469 heavy rounds fired. The 3rd Battle Cruiser Squadron, the beneficiary of gunnery practice immediately before the battle, scored a more impressive 4.29 per cent. British battleship gunnery was also mediocre. The heavily engaged 5th Battle Squadron scored an overall accuracy of 2.64 per cent (29 out of 1,099) while the dreadnoughts of the Grand Fleet combined for a 3.70 per cent accuracy rate (57 of 1,593). Of note, several divisions of dreadnoughts were hardly able to engage at all. The division, composed of *King George V, Ajax, Centurion* and *Erin*, fired a total of only 34 rounds in the entire battle, with *Erin* firing none. Another division of four Orion-class units fired just less than 200 rounds.

The British system of central direction proved its worth, but the standard 9ft rangefinder was generally inadequate and the rapid changes in range, combined with poor visibility, were too much for the Dreyer Table plotting system. The relatively primitive German fire-control system worked well under the conditions, and the German stereoscopic rangefinder proved better than the British coincidence instruments.

The real lesson of the battle was the fact that it was extremely difficult to sink a dreadnought by gunfire. Even the less-armoured battlecruisers were heavily resistant to gunfire. The ability of the German battlecruisers to receive damage was outstanding, for they were armoured about as well as some British dreadnoughts. It was not their poor armour that doomed the three British battlecruisers lost at Jutland, but rather the character of British ammunition powder. Unlike German powder, when British powder was ignited it burned quickly and created intense over-pressures. To complete the potential for disaster, British flash doors fitted to protect powder in the magazine and in the hoist to the turret were not adequately tested before the war, and proved

Hits on battleships and battlecruisers

Battleships		Total hits by heavy shells
British	*Barham*	6
	Warspite	15
	Malaya	7
	Colossus	2
German	*König*	10
	Grosser Kurfürst	8
	Markgraf	5
	Kaiser	2
	Helgoland	1
Battlecruisers		
British	*Lion*	13
	Princess Royal	9
	Queen Mary	7
	Tiger	15
	New Zealand	1
	Indefatigable	5
	Invincible	5
German	*Lutzow*	24
	Derfflinger	21
	Seydlitz	22
	Moltke	5
	Von der Tann	4

Seydlitz was hit by an amazing total of 21 heavy shells and one torpedo during the battle of Jutland, but survived to return home, although as shown here she was barely afloat. She survived the war only to be scuttled in June 1919.

unable to withstand the violent reaction of the powder when ignited. When the flash of ignited powder reached the ship's magazine, it produced complete destruction.

All three battlecruisers, as well as the two armoured cruisers that blew up, were lost in the same way. It is true that British gunnery practices at Jutland kept a greater number of powder charges out of the magazine at any given time to increase the rate of fire, but this was only a contributing factor.

In 1914, the Germans generally took less care than the British with precautions for flash protection. Such was shown during the battle of Dogger Bank, when a 13.5in shell hit and penetrated the aft turret barbette of *Seydlitz*. A total of 62 charges totalling more than six tons of powder ignited and burned, but did not explode like British powder would have. The Germans did not introduce flash precautions because of this

Despite the ten hits from British heavy shells, *König* was never in any danger of sinking. Repairs took until 21 July 1916 to complete. Some of the internal damage is shown here, but casualties were relatively light at 45 dead and 27 wounded.

incident before Jutland. They did limit the number of charges out of the magazine at any one time, but overall their magazines were not flash tight. The saving grace for the Germans was that their powder charges burned relatively slowly when ignited, and did not cause the dangerous pressure rise created by British powder.

Another factor reducing the effectiveness of British gunnery was the performance of its shells. British shells tended to break up when striking heavy armour at an oblique angle, and detonated before penetrating deep into the plate. The defects of British armour-piercing shells ranged from the use of lyddite as a bursting agent to shells being too brittle and fuses that had no delay. Of the 13 heavy shells that hit German armour 10in thick or more, only six were effective. British shells also performed poorly against armour of only 6–9in.

AFTERMATH

In the aftermath of the great battle, the German propaganda machine went into high gear to paint the engagement as a German victory. On 5 June, only four days after the return of the High Seas Fleet to Wilhelmshaven, the Kaiser made an appearance at the naval base to award decorations and to promote Scheer to fleet admiral. Given the high expectations created by the High Seas Fleet's performance, the Germans could not give up on future operations in the North Sea. Despite popular belief, the High Seas Fleet continued to challenge the Royal Navy in the North Sea after Jutland.

As soon as the fleet was ready for action, Scheer planned another bombardment of the English coast. Learning from the lessons of Jutland, Scheer paid particular attention to the co-ordination of his Zeppelin and U-boat arms to avoid being surprised again. The slow pre-dreadnoughts were left behind and Hipper's battlecruisers were augmented by three dreadnoughts.

The High Seas Fleet sortied on the night of 18 August. Just as in the hours before Jutland, British intelligence had alerted Jellicoe to the German sortie and the Grand

Flagship of the Grand Fleet *Queen Elizabeth* pictured on 21 November 1918, steaming off Scapa Flow as the High Seas Fleet is about to be interned.

76

Fleet put to sea to intercept. The actual event was anti-climactic. The dreadnought *Westfalen* was torpedoed by a British submarine on 19 August and a variety of reports from submarines and Zeppelins, combined with radio intelligence, confirmed to Scheer that the Grand Fleet was at sea. A similar operation planned for September was cancelled due to poor weather.

In October, the U-boats were pulled away to participate in the latest round of on-again, off-again commerce raiding. Their absence made Scheer even more cautious by limiting operations to the central and eastern parts of the North Sea. When the High Seas Fleet sortied on 10 and 19 October, these operations did not even draw a reaction from the British.

Ironically, the greatest success of the High Seas Fleet after Jutland would be in the Baltic Sea, long a naval backwater. By late 1917, the Russian Army was cracking apart and the Germans advancing up the Baltic coast. To use the port of Riga as a supply base, the Germans had to take the Russian-held islands in the Gulf of Riga. In order to accomplish this objective, one battlecruiser and ten dreadnoughts of the High Seas Fleet were committed to support the operation. From 12 to 20 October, the Germans cleared the Russians from the Gulf of Riga and established German maritime dominance in the Baltic.

The last major German surface operation of the war was conducted in April 1918, when Hipper led his battlecruisers, supported by the dreadnoughts, on a raid against one of the Norway-to-Britain convoys. The operation ended in a fiasco when a British submarine torpedoed a battlecruiser already crippled by engineering problems. In the last weeks of the war, Hipper, now commander of the High Seas Fleet, was preparing a major fleet sortie into the North Sea that had all the earmarks of a death ride. On 27 October, units of the High Seas Fleet, long suffering from bad morale brought on primarily by inactivity, refused to accept orders. Within days, the mutiny had spread throughout the fleet.

According to the terms of the Armistice effective on 11 November 1918, the cream of the High Seas Fleet was to be interned at Scapa Flow. Accordingly, on 21 November, nine of the most modern German dreadnoughts, five battlecruisers, seven light cruisers and 49 destroyers were escorted by the Grand Fleet into custody. In May 1919, the once-proud German dreadnoughts and the rest of the fleet scuttled themselves in Scapa Flow, marking the end of the High Seas Fleet.

The Bayern class was a larger version of the König class, and was armed with 15in guns. A lack of speed made her the equivalent of the British Revenge class. *Bayern* was operational at the time of Jutland, but was left behind because her crew was not considered fully trained. Here she is shown sinking by the stern on 21 June 1919, when the Germans scuttled the units surrendered at Scapa Flow.

FURTHER READING

Bonney, George, *The Battle of Jutland 1916*, Sutton Publishing, Phoenix Mill (2002)

Breyer, Siegfried, *Battleships and Battlecruisers 1905–1970*, Doubleday and Company, Garden City, NY (1973)

Brooks, John, 'The Mast and Funnel Question: Fire-control Positions in British Dreadnoughts 1905–1915' in *Warship 1995*, Conway Maritime Press, London (1995)

Burt, R. A., *British Battleships of World War One*, Naval Institute Press, Annapolis, MD (1986)

Campbell, John, *Jutland: An Analysis of the Fighting*, Lyons Press, NY (1998)

Campbell, John, 'German Dreadnoughts and their Protection' in *Warship*, Vol. I, Naval Institute Press, Annapolis, MD (1977)

Corbett, Julian S., *Naval Operations*, Vol. III, The Naval and Military Press, Uckfield, nd

Fawcett, H.W. and G.W.W. Hooper, *The Fighting at Jutland*, Naval Institute Press, Annapolis, MD (2001)

Friedman, Norman, *Naval Firepower*, Naval Institute Press, Annapolis, MD (2008)

Friedman, Norman, *Battleship: Design and Development 1905–1945*, Mayflower Books, NY (1978)

Gardiner, Robert (ed.), *The Eclipse of the Big Gun*, Naval Institute Press, Annapolis, MD (1992)

Gordon, Andrew, *The Rules of the Game*, Naval Institute Press, Annapolis, MD (2000)

Gregor, Rene, *Battleships of the World*, Naval Institute Press, Annapolis, MD (1997)

Halpern, Paul G., *A Naval History of World War I*, Naval Institute Press, Annapolis, MD (1994)

Hart, Nigel and Peter, *Jutland 1916*, Cassell, London (2003)

Herwig, Holger H., *'Luxury Fleet'*, The Ashfield Press, London (1991)

Hodges, Peter, *The Big Gun*, Naval Institute Press, Annapolis, MD (1981)

Ireland, Bernard, *Jane's Battleships of the 20th Century*, HarperCollins, NY (1996)

London, Charles, *Jutland 1916*, Osprey Publishing, Oxford (2000)

Marder, Arthur, *From the Dreadnought to Scapa Flow*, Vol. III, *Jutland and After*, Oxford University Press, London (1966)

Massie, Robert, *Castles of Steel*, Random House, NY (2003)

McCallum, Iain, 'The Riddle of the Shells, 1914–18: Disappointment in the North Sea' in *Warship 2005*, Conway Maritime Press, London (2005)

Philbin, Tobias III, *SMS König* (Warship Profile 37), Profile Publications Limited, Windsor (1973)

Preston, Antony, *Battleships of World War I*, Stackpole Books, Harrisburg, PA (1972)

Scheer, Reinhard, *Germany's High Seas Fleet in the World War*, The Battery Press, Nashville, TN (2002)

Tarrant, V.E., *Jutland: The German Perspective*, Naval Institute Press, Annapolis, MD (1995)

Wingate, John, 'HMS Dreadnought' in *Warships in Profile*, Vol. 1, Profile Publications Limited, Windsor (1971)

Wragg, David, *Royal Navy Handbook 1914–1918*, Sutton Publishing, Phoenix Mill (2006)

Yates, Keith, *Flawed Victory*, Naval Institute Press, Annapolis, MD (2000)

INDEX